Richard's exposition of Scripture
contains wisdom from decades of s
while serving God's people. This inviting, rich work is for pastors,
laypersons, and everyone else in between.

—**Aaron Campbell**
Lead pastor of Antioch Christian Fellowship, Philadelphia
Executive director of Level Up Philly
Author (*Eyes That Seen Plenty*)

Pastor Richard Cimino provides us with a fresh, refreshing and,
most importantly, a sound biblical look at our identity in Christ.
Because our identity impacts the way we view God and the world
around us this book will prove to be a useful tool to every Christian
and Christian leader.

—**Jim Gallagher**
Senior Pastor Calvary Vero Beach

No question is more crucial in today's culture than *Who am I?*
It is the question of identity in a world where so many have no
trustworthy family or institutions to help them. That leaves
people to search inside for those answers, a sure road to anxiety
and emptiness. Richard Cimino brings decades of exceptional
pastoral and expositional experience to show us a better way to
find solid foundation for a Jesus centered identity. It is a must read!

—**Gerry Breshears, Ph.D.**
Professor of Theology
Western Seminary, Portland

Richard writes, speaks, and lives a life soaked in grace. This beautiful book invites us to consider what it means to live fully in and for Christ. His authentic and practical understanding of the power of the Gospel radiates from every page.

—**Sarah Yardley**
Mission and Ministry Lead, Creation Fest UK,
Author and Friend

Paul's letter to the Ephesians is one of my favorite portions of Scripture. It is also an extremely relevant text in relation to many of the perplexing issues of the day. One issue in particular addressed in Ephesians is that of identity. It seems that the culture is in the midst of a collective identity crises and no one knows where to turn to find the answer. Paul's answer is that our true identity can only be found in one place—in Christ. In this book, Richard Cimino, with great expository skill and pastoral insight takes us deep into the heart of Ephesians to discover that what truly defines us is nothing less than the love of Christ that is wider, longer, higher and deeper than our minds can grasp, yet revealed to us who are in Christ by his Spirit.

—**Brian Brodersen**
Pastor, Calvary Chapel Costa Mesa,
California

Richard Cimino understands something that eludes Christians, the question of knowing who I am is never adequately answered when the beginning point is me. As he points out, humans are created as relational beings who only have clarity about who they are and where they fit in when viewing themselves as God intended—a created person in relationship with a Creator, a broken person in relationship with a Healer, a corrupted person in relationship with a Redeemer. He then takes the reader on a journey aimed at discovering each aspect of the self as it can only be truly known through the lens of a relationship with Christ. Further, Pastor Cimino points the reader to the remarkable way in which every question a person poses about who they are and where they fit is made sensible by the gospel of the sin atoning work of Jesus. The work of a teacher is to take grand sweeping biblical truths and demonstrate how when applied they transform the heart. I think *Who Am I* takes a giant step in this direction.

—Jeffrey S. Black, Ph.D.
Professor, Department of Counseling & Psychology
Licensed Psychologist
Cairn University

I have known Pastor Richard for many years. Ever since I have known Richard he has had a love for God's Word and a great desire to proclaim the gospel. I have been so blessed to see him grow into one the finest bible teachers I know. Our community is encouraged each day as his teaching is broadcast on our local Christian radio station WRDJ.

Pastor Richard's commentary in the wonderful book of Ephesians is an excellent thorough exposition of this section of scripture. He reminds us of who we are, who we can be, and that our true identity is to be found "in Christ." I can assure the reader that this is not merely head knowledge for the author—it is something he believes and lives.

—Malcolm Wild
Senior Pastor Calvary Chapel Merritt Island, Florida

One of the most important books in the New Testament for a follower of Jesus to read, know and understand is the book of Ephesians. In *Who I Am*, Pastor Richard Cimino does a masterful job of unpacking the deep theological truths concerning our identity in Christ. Along with these deep theological truths are practical insights that bring to life what it means to walk with Jesus and live a victorious Christian life.

—Rob Salvato
Lead Pastor at Calvary Vista in Vista, California

"In a generation of identity crisis this book helps realign our hearts with who we are and who we are not in light of who we were created to be. Dive into discovering who you truly are today according to scriptures through your journey in the book of Ephesians."

—Pastor Ray Dash
The Rock Christian Fellowship

The exacting question "Who am I in Christ?" is as pertinent today as it was for the early believers in Ephesus. Richard's examination is a worthwhile read for those learning to live through and for Jesus Christ.'

—Nathan S. McConnell
Minister, Downfield Mains Church,
Dundee, Scotland

who i am

receiving the identity
we could never create

richard cimino

CLAY BRIDGES
P R E S S

Who I Am: Receiving the Identity We Could Never Create

eISBN: 978-1-68488-041-6
ISBN: 978-1-68488-040-9

For Valerie

You have loved me faithfully, courageously, graciously, tenderly and relentlessly for 45 years. During many of those years you got the worst version of me as I tried to create my identity based on the things I did for Jesus. To top it all off you've cheered me on while I worked on a book that describes the man I should have been for you. You are absolutely amazing!
I pray that you will reap from my life a massive harvest from all the love, grace and mercy you have sown into it.
Amoré Amoré Amoré

For Deborah, Sean, Ashley, and Nathan

Each of you are so bright—so beautiful—so uniquely gifted. Thank you for always saying, "Love you so much!"
I don't know if you know this, but you always make me feel like I'm your hero and that leaves me wrecked in the most glorious way.

special thanks to

Malcolm Wild for being a mentor, music maker, missionary and friend.

You took risks by giving me opportunities to minister. Looking back, I know I was a handful.

I'm sure I took years off your life.

Brian Brodersen for being such a great friend, a great listener. Thanks for those countless conversations in which we hammered out ideas and opinions. When I walked away from those conversations I would find myself thinking, "Brian and I are so much alike—only Brian's way nicer!"

Travis Clark for being such a great man, husband, dad, pastor, assistant and friend.

You make me wish I could have a do-over.

John Hwang for being more than a friend. There's way more to say than there is space to write. Thanks for being like a loving son to Valerie and me and big brother to Deborah, Sean, Ashley and Nathan.

Paul Tripp for telling me that I had to write a book. But even more, thank you for investing in my life when at the very time you have more on your plate than ever before. Thank you for reminding me that "Jesus is worth it."

table of contents

WHO I AM:
Receiving the Identity I Could Never Create

introduction

Who am I? All of us have asked that question. It's a huge one!

Every culture has a very definite grid through which they try to derive their identity—their most profound sense of meaning.

> *You are what you do.*
> *You are what you have.*
> *You are who you know.*
> *You are where you live.*
> *You are what you drive.*
> *You are what you wear.*

It's safe to say that *everything* broken in culture had its beginning with an *identity crisis.* Our first parents were supposed to be defined by their relationship to their loving Creator. They were made to convey and reflect the image and glory of God. Everything broken in the world is rooted in the moment when humans chose to believe the lie of lies—that we can find meaning and identity from something other than God, from created things rather than the Creator.

1

Genesis 3 records how our first parents rejected their true identities. Rather than find their true identity in conveying the image of God, reflecting the glory of God and living for the glory of God, they sought to establish an identity that was rooted in their independence from God and in the pursuit of their own glory. Everything that is broken in this world is traced back to this crisis of identity.

That decision, in the words of John Lennox, "triggered such a seismic catastrophe, from which the world has been reeling ever since."[1] That is why we need to be rescued. Lennox went on to write:

> Sin entered the world to wreak endless havoc. So serious is that moral infection that the business of restoring men and women to fellowship with their Creator will involve something much bigger than creation itself: nothing less than the Creator becoming human, dying at the hands of his creatures and rising again in triumph over sin and death.[2]

The world is a mess today because ever since Genesis 3, every man and woman has been following in the footsteps of their first parents, seeking to define themselves by something other than God. We are always concerned with our identity. We are always trying to find, as Paul Tripp put it, our "replacement identity."

Follow me here! God made us to reflect His glory and bring Him glory by being fruitful and productive. Instead, we look to our productivity and success to provide identity, meaning, and purpose. Here's the truth: you are *not* what you do.

---

1. John C. Lennox, *Seven Days That Divide the World* (Grand Rapids, MI: Zondervan, 2011),.
2. Ibid.

God also intended us to reflect His glory and bring Him glory by living in meaningful, loving relationships and community with one another. Loving relationships are very important in the eyes of God. Jesus said the greatest commandment is to love the Lord your God with all your heart, soul, and mind, and the second is to love one another (Matt. 22:37–39).

But here's the deal. Relationships were never designed or intended to give us our identity. When we seek to derive the deepest sense of who we are from our relationships, we are headed for disaster because we are looking to people to give us what only God can give. Sooner or later, like any and every created thing, people will fail us. By the way, when you look to a relationship to define you, to supply you with your identity, you're not really loving that person. You're loving you. Instead of serving and loving people because they reflect the image and glory of our loving Creator, you're using them for the sense of identity you're longing for.

Don't miss this! In reality, those relationships become our functional savior. We look to them to save us from a life without meaning. No friendship, no marriage, and no child can bear up under the weight of being your savior. They will be crushed under that weight, and they will always disappoint you.

God created a perfect world for our first parents to enjoy. In a sense, God said, "Here's the world! It's yours to enjoy. Take care of it for me, and reflect my glory in the way you use this perfectly designed world." Amazingly, the first man and woman rejected their identities as stewards and tenants of God's world. Ever since Genesis 3, people have been trying to find their identity in what part of the world they possess. World wars have been fought over it. People have been murdered for "stuff." What we have seems to define us on our journey to find our identity.

3

It's not a sin to have things, purchase things, appreciate quality and craftsmanship, and enjoy things. But when things become the source of our identity, we are substituting those things for God, and *that* is idolatry.

The list of replacement identities is long. We see them all around us. They shape lives, and they shape the world we live in. People define themselves by their ethnicity, their sexual orientation, their political affiliation, and their hobbies. Then, to protect and reinforce their false identity, they seek to be part of a collection of others who share the same replacement identity. Some people refer to these groups as tribes. They make an idol of their tribe and demonize other tribes. Democrats demonize Republicans, and vice versa. The Raider Nation demonizes Bronco fans, and vice versa.

Life without Jesus is exhausting! Before coming to Jesus, we are always trying to find our replacement identity, and then we try to protect, preserve, and enhance that identity. Life without Jesus consists of nonstop, moment-by-moment concern with "How will this make me look? What will I get out of this? How will this make me feel more secure about who I am?"

Before coming to know Jesus, I lived for and served anything and everything that gave me the identity I wanted, the identity I desperately needed. Above all, it was the identity that a fallen culture would acknowledge and approve of. I was a slave to the identity system of fallen culture and its demands on me. Simply put, life before Jesus was all about who I am. All of that is behind the question "Who am I?"

That's the groundwork concerning our great struggle for meaning—the identity crisis that has left every man and woman utterly broken and every culture strewn with the wreckage produced by everyone's substitute identities.

But here is the good news! From Genesis 3 and throughout all 39 books of the Old Testament is the story of God's relentless, rescuing love. In each of those 39 books, God promised, pointed to, and anticipated the coming of the One who would make a way for us to be reconciled to God and restored to our original and true identity.

In those 39 books we discover that God not only promised to rescue us but never flinched in the face of man's rebellion. God was relentless in His rescuing love. Throughout thousands of years of human history in the face of mankind's insistence on finding their deepest sense of meaning in anything and everything other than the true and living God, our God never stopped speaking. He constantly moved forward, making and fulfilling promise after promise. He faithfully directed the affairs of human history so at a specific moment in time He would come in human flesh, live the life we could not live, die the death we should have died, and rise again to conquer death and guarantee our redemption.

Finally, after the Old Testament, which was a foreshadowing of our rescue, our Redeemer became substance in the first four books of the New Testament. Those books are called the Gospels. Gospel means the announcement of news. It is the record of something that has happened. Those first four books are about *Someone* who did *something*. Mark's Gospel opens with these words: "The beginning of the gospel of Jesus Christ, the Son of God" (Mark 1:1).

The solution to our search for identity and meaning is a Person. The answer to our question *Who am I?* is answered in a Person.

Who Jesus is and what He has done to save us changes everything.

For you know that God paid a ransom to save you
from the empty life you inherited from your ancestors.
And it was not paid with mere gold or silver, which

lose their value. It was the precious blood of Christ, the sinless, spotless Lamb of God. God chose him as your ransom long before the world began, but now in these last days he has been revealed for your sake. Through Christ you have come to trust in God.

—1 Pet. 1:18–21 NLT

Because of the cross and resurrection of Jesus and because of all God did to rescue me, I am so certain of God's great love for me that I have the freedom and the courage not to be concerned about myself in moments that previously would have been all about me. The question is no longer "How will this make me look? What will I get out of this? How will this make me feel more secure about who I am?" The question is this: "How will this moment make Jesus look great? How will this success, this relationship, or this treasure bring Jesus glory? How will this success, this relationship, or this treasure point others to Jesus so they might be rescued?"

Let's make a couple of observations and ask some hard questions.

Observation: Many people go to church not because they see God and His glory as the source of their true identity or because they want to learn about how to best convey the image of God for the glory of God. They go because they're actually hoping that Jesus will help them build their false identity. They want Jesus and the church to give them the marriage that will define them, the sense of belonging they want, or the success they desire. They believe that the point of church is to leave them feeling better about and more secure in their replacement identity. That's why so many churches have such a large variety of affinity groups that are built around and cater to replacement identities.

How about the issue of identity and prayer? The prayer life of the average professing Christian today is a laundry list of things they believe are necessary in order for their lives to have meaning and happiness. But Jesus taught that real prayer begins with recognizing God's glory and being concerned that His will be done on earth for His glory.

Why is it that many men and women who believe with their hearts in the Lord Jesus and believe that because of the cross and His resurrection they've been rescued and are going to heaven still struggle with anxiety, fear, and insecurities?

Christians, we (including me) need to hear this. We have not just been rescued from the eternal consequences of sin and idolatry to a forever in the presence of God, but we have been given a new identity. Pastor and author Paul Tripp said, "Because we have been rescued by the death and resurrection of Jesus, we not only have a new destiny—we have a new identity."

That brings us to the next bit of groundwork. The first four books of the New Testament are the Holy Spirit's inspired record of the life and mission of Jesus, including His virgin birth, His sinless life, His death on a cross, and His bodily resurrection from the grave three days later. By way of the 21 books of the New Testament, called epistles, the Holy Spirit unpacks the record of the life and mission of Jesus. They explain how any and all who believe with their heart on the Lord Jesus can be saved.

These letters explain how believers enjoy and foster a vertical relationship with their Redeemer, become a brand new person, and receive a new identity that's rooted in Jesus. They explain how a believer's new and true identity defines and directs them in the way they live horizontally in relationship with others who have put their faith in Jesus and in relationship with a world that so desperately needs to be redeemed. They explain how that new identity and way of living will meet opposition and how they can stand in the face of it.

If all the New Testament letters do that, why single out Ephesians? After all, the Bible is all inspired (God-breathed)—not just the ideas but the very words. The shortest book of the Bible (3 John) has only 219 words in the original language, but it is just as inspired as the longest book of the Bible (Jeremiah) with its 33,002 words.

The collection of these 66 divinely inspired books is like a mountain range with each book a peak in the range. But in a mountain range there are some peaks that rise higher than others. In a sense that is true in the mountain range of inspired Scripture. The heights of the Old Testament are amazing, but they point to and promise the heights of the Gospels where we have a record of the revelation of God in the person of Jesus. The prologue of John's Gospel is staggering in the heights it takes us. In the span of 18 verses we are told that Jesus is the Word of God and the pre-existent, all-powerful God of creation who left the glory of heaven and stepped into human flesh.

> *And the Word became flesh and dwelt among us, and we have seen his glory, glory as of the only Son from the Father, full of grace and truth. For from his fullness we have all received, grace upon grace. For the law was given through Moses; grace and truth came through Jesus Christ. No one has ever seen God; the only God, who is at the Father's side, he has made him known.*
> —John 1:14, 16–18

These words are among the highest peaks in all of Scripture. Mount Everest is the highest peak on the planet. K2 is a close second, less than 1,000 feet shorter. Ephesians is the Everest or the K2 of the New Testament. Martyn Lloyd-Jones said, "Ephesians is the most sublime and majestic expression of the gospel."[3] John Stott wrote, "The letter to the Ephesians is a marvellously concise, yet comprehensive, summary of the Christian good news and its implications. Nobody can read it without being moved by to wonder and worship, and challenged to consistency of life."[4]

From the vantage point of this letter we get a breathtaking view of all God has done for us. It's also been called the Grand Canyon of Scripture because in it we see the depth and breadth and length and height of God's love and mercy in His plan of salvation. Then it sets forth with simplicity and clarity how the redeemed life connects the already and the not yet. The flow of this letter moves from the theological to the practical.

In the first three chapters, Paul, the writer of the letter, presents all God has done for us in, through, with, and by Jesus. And woven into that stunning theology is the portrait of our new and true identity. We see who we are because of all God has done for us.

In Ephesians 4:1–6:9, Paul tells us that who we are in Jesus determines how we live for Jesus. The life, death, and resurrection of Jesus can never go without response. There is a way of living attached to the rescued life. It's not the drudgery of a religious life but the responsibilities of the redeemed life that are seen as privilege and undertaken out of love for Jesus. As we will see in this letter, Paul is saying something like this: "Look at these responsibilities. What a privilege to undertake these responsibilities out of love for the One who loved you and gave Himself for you!"

Finally, in Ephesians 6:10 Paul makes it clear that who we are in Jesus and how we live for Jesus in a broken world will always be met with very real spiritual opposition. Wow! In this one amazing

---

3. David Martyn Lloyd-Jones, *God's Ultimate Purpose: An Exposition of Ephesians One* (Carlisle, PA: Banner of Truth, 1978), 12.

4. John R. W. Stott, *God's New Society: The Message of Ephesians* (Downers Grove, IL: InterVarsity Press, 1979), 15.

letter, I discover who I am in Jesus, how I live for Jesus, and how I stand for Jesus.

In this book, we're going to take a deep dive into the first three chapters of Ephesians. Those three chapters unfold and paint for us a detailed portrait of the identity we could never create.

That portrait begins to unfold in the life of the author of the letter. His story is an object lesson in how we are deeply and tragically invested in creating identities that are empty and how Jesus rescues us from them and supplies each of us with our true and forever identity.

Here we go!

chapter one

the man who wrote the letter

W e've now laid out the groundwork for our study of the first three chapters of Ephesians. It started with the observation that all of us at one time or another in one way or another have asked the question, "Who am I?" The second observation was that every culture has a very definite grid through which people try to derive their identity—their deepest sense of meaning. Fallen humanity desperately needs to be rescued from *acts* and *consequences* (temporal and eternal) of trying to find meaning and identity from something other than God.

The Bible not only tells *why* we are broken but *how* we can be rescued and made whole. Jesus becomes our magnificent obsession (to borrow the title of David Robertson's book). We have been rescued from the eternal consequences of sin and idolatry to a forever in the presence of God.

Here we go!

*Paul, an apostle of Christ Jesus by the will of God,
to the saints who are in Ephesus, and are faithful in
Christ Jesus.*

—Eph. 1:1

The author of this letter is a man named Paul (previously called Saul). In his own words he tells us that before meeting Jesus, he looked to his ethnicity, education, and religion to define his identity and derive his deepest sense of meaning. He said he was circumcised on the eighth day and was of the people of Israel, of the tribe of Benjamin, a Hebrew of Hebrews. He was carefully trained in Jewish laws and customs in Jerusalem at the feet of Gamaliel, the greatest teacher in Israel. He advanced beyond his peers academically. He lived as a Pharisee, the strictest sect in Judaism. Regarding the outward adherence to the Law of God, Paul said he was blameless.

Paul was a man who was heavily invested in his replacement identities. Jesus was a threat to everything Paul had previously used to define himself and supply his deepest sense of meaning. And isn't that true for all of us? Along with that, the person whose significance and security are deeply rooted in Jesus poses a threat to our replacement identities. The message of the gospel and the life of the authentic Christian tell us what we already know: *we are deeply and tragically invested in identities that are empty.*

That's why Paul (when he was called Saul) hated Jesus. That's why he hated the message about Jesus. That's why he hated those who loved Jesus and proclaimed Jesus as the Messiah of Israel and Savior of the world. In his own words, he said he was filled with "raging fury" (Acts 26:11) against them. In order to protect our replacement identity, we have to endlessly work to preserve and enhance that identity. To do that we seek to be part of a collection of others who share the same replacement identity; we find our "tribe." We make an idol of that tribe and demonize other tribes. That was exactly the case with Paul.

> *I persecuted this Way to the death, binding and delivering to prison both men and women, as the high priest and the whole council of elders can bear me witness. From them I received letters to the brothers, and I journeyed toward Damascus to take those also who were there and bring them in bonds to Jerusalem to be punished.*
>
> —Acts 22:4–5

Paul became the architect of a systematic, relentless, organized, and violent persecution of the gospel. In his own words, he "persecuted the church of God violently and tried to destroy it" (Gal. 1:13). But there came a day—a day when Paul was on his way to the city of Damascus, filled with a maniacal rage against everything and everyone that had to do with Jesus—that he met the Jesus he hated. He discovered that the Jesus he hated loved him! While he was relentlessly persecuting those who loved Jesus, Jesus was relentlessly chasing Paul.

> *There is more grace in the heart of God than there is sin in the heart of man.*
>
> —Tim Chaddick

A light from heaven suddenly flashed around Paul, who fell to the ground and said, "Who are you?" The answer shocked him! From that blinding light the voice said, "I am Jesus!" That was the very name Paul had hated and persecuted. He would have buried it forever if he could have. Jesus said something like this: "Paul, your war against the Christians is really a war against me!" We need to understand that we declare war against God when our identity is based on independence from God. Jesus said something like this: "Paul, that fight is unreasonable! That fight is self-destructive."

This blows my mind! Jesus was the one under attack yet He was concerned about how hard it was for Paul to be fighting against grace.

Paul was utterly undone by Jesus.

> *I used to blaspheme the name of Christ. In my insolence, I persecuted his people. But God had mercy on me. . . . Oh, how generous and gracious our Lord was! . . . This is a trustworthy saying, and everyone should accept it: "Christ Jesus came into the world to save sinners"—and I am the worst of them all. But God had mercy on me so that Christ Jesus could use me as a prime example of his great patience with even the worst sinners.*
>
> —1 Tim. 1:13–16 NLT

In the face of the love and patience and mercy of Jesus, Paul discovered that everything he treasured and looked to for identity was worthless. Here's how he put it in one of his other letters:

> *But whatever gain I had, I counted as loss for the sake of Christ. Indeed, I count everything as loss because of the surpassing worth of knowing Christ Jesus my Lord. For his sake I have suffered the loss of all things and count them as rubbish, in order that I may gain Christ.*
>
> —Phil. 3:7–8

From that moment on, Paul's identity was no longer wrapped up in race, education, or dead religion. It was wrapped up in the grace of God and his relationship with God because of grace. It was wrapped up in the will of God and the glory of God.

Before meeting Jesus, Paul wasted his life seeking to derive his identity through his status and prominence in Judaism. But Paul began his letter to the Christians at Ephesus by saying that the weight and prestige of being an apostle in the church was not the thing that defined him or gave meaning to his life. His countless travels and exploits as an apostle were not the things that defined him. The only reason he mentioned those things was because they were tied to Jesus Christ and the will of God. His identity was not rooted in being an apostle. His identity was rooted in his life being connected to Jesus and the will of God.

The book of Ephesians begins with these words: "Paul, an apostle of Christ Jesus by the will of God." Here's a little exercise. Put your name in place of Paul's. Then instead of the word *apostle*, write whatever your job title is or whatever it is you do. Mine would read, "Richard, a husband by the will of God; Richard, a dad by the will of God; Richard, a pastor by the will of God." Yours might read, "_____, a student by the will of God." "_____, a housewife by the will of God." "_____, a dentist by the will of God." The world says that the source of your identity is the thing you wrote instead of the word *apostle*. But the Bible says the source of your identity is "the will of God." Maybe you're a housewife and a mom by the will of God. The world says you have an identity problem if you're stuck at the kitchen sink or in the laundry room. The world says you need to get out of the house and make something of yourself if you're ever going to find meaning.

Paul says no, his new and true identity is tied to Jesus, not to what he has done. Jesus became the source of Paul's significance and security. Whatever it is that He wants me to do and wherever it is that He wants me to go, it has significance because it is for Jesus.

chapter two

true identity starts here

To the saints who are in Ephesus, and are faithful in Christ Jesus.

—Eph. 1:1

This is the first element of our new and true identity. The little phrase "in Christ Jesus" is theologically profound. It's at the heart of why this letter is, as Martyn Lloyd-Jones said, "the most sublime and majestic expression of the gospel." It's why it's such a marvelously concise yet comprehensive summary of the Christian good news and its implications.

In this short letter, the phrase "in Christ" appears 13 times; "in Christ Jesus" appears eight times; and "in him" appears eight times.

Draw a circle. Next to the circle write "Jesus." Place a dot in the center of the circle. Label the dot "Me."

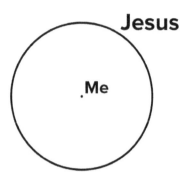

You used to be outside of Jesus. But the moment you believe with your heart on the Lord Jesus Christ, a miracle takes place. You are placed *into* Jesus. "In Christ" is one of the most significant outcomes of the sinless life, sacrificial death, and bodily resurrection of Jesus.

What are the implications of this identity for the believer? It means that as a Christian, you have two addresses. You have a geographical address ("to the saints who are in Ephesus"), but you also have a spiritual address. No matter where you might be on planet earth, you literally live "in Christ."

To be in Jesus is to be totally identified with Jesus. I'll try to illustrate. Take an M&M. Hold it. It has its own unique identity—a specific size, shape, and color. But once you eat that M&M, it loses its identity. It is totally assimilated into who you are. When someone looks at you, they don't see the M&M; they see you.

We are, by faith in the gospel, utterly and forever identified with Jesus. What are the implications of that? Every element of our relationship to God found in the first three chapters of Ephesians is secured and experienced because by faith we are identified with Jesus.

Chosen in Christ (1:4)
Adopted in Christ (1:5)
Blessed in Christ (1:6)
Redeemed in Christ (1:7)

Forgiven in Christ (1:7)
Made known His will in Christ (1:9)
Given an inheritance in Christ (1:11)
Glorified in Christ (1:12)
Granted hope in Christ (1:18)
Given power in Christ (1:19–20)
Made alive in Christ (2:5–6)
Brought near to God in Christ (2:13)
Connected with other believers in Christ (2:21)
Built together in Christ (2:22)
Partakers of His promise in Christ (3:6)
Granted boldness and access through faith in Christ (3:12)

It is in Christ that we receive and enjoy the abundant life He died for us to have. It doesn't matter what your geographical location is. It doesn't matter what your circumstances are. None of that can diminish or rob you of that abundant life because wherever you are and whatever your circumstances, you are "in Christ Jesus."

Another amazing outcome of being in Christ is that because you are in Christ, nothing can touch you unless it passes through Jesus. Adversity, trial, or persecution can only touch us by permission of Jesus.

Christian, say this out loud: *I am in Christ.*

Let's look at Ephesians 1:1 again: "To the saints who are in Ephesus." The word *saint* means "one who has been set apart." It is related to the word *sanctified*, which means "set apart"—set apart to God and for God, which is exactly the original identity of mankind. Humans were made by God and for God's purposes and glory. Being a saint (near to God as a unique instrument for His glory) is not the result of something you and I accomplish. It's not something we cease being because of our failures. This identity—being a saint—is the outcome of being rescued.

The out-of-pocket cost for you and me to be saints is *zero*. But it cost God everything to rescue you and me from the utterly futile and fatal efforts to find our identity apart from Him. Anyone who trusts in the death and resurrection of Jesus to save them is a saint. Nine times in this brief letter, Paul addresses his readers as saints (Eph. 1:1, 15, 18, 2:19, 3:8, 18, 4:12, 5:3, 6:18). Saint is not a title. It is an identity. It is a position of nearness to God that we did not earn. We are set apart to God and for God because we are in Jesus.

Christian, say this out loud with me: *I am a saint.*

Ephesians 1:2 says, "Grace to you and peace from God our Father and the Lord Jesus Christ." We find these two words— *grace* and *peace*—in every epistle. When God repeats Himself, pay attention. They are like inseparable twins. Grace is always first, even the three times He says grace, mercy, and peace. Why?

Grace = God giving to us what we don't deserve, what we could never earn. It is grace that paves the way for every blessing we receive from Him, especially the blessing of peace. God's grace *must* always come before peace.

> *The carnal [unbelieving] mind is enmity against God.*
> —Rom. 8:7 KJV

> *Alienated and enemies in your mind by wicked works.*
> —Col. 1:21 KJV

While alienated from God, we deserved judgment—"the wages of sin is death" (Rom. 6:23). In that state we deserved wrath—we "were by nature children of wrath" (Eph. 2:3). But when we were His enemies, deserving judgment and wrath, He gave us something we did not deserve.

For God so loved the world, that he gave his only begotten Son, that whosoever believeth in him should not perish, but have everlasting life.

—John 3:16 KJV

But God commendeth his love toward us, in that, while we were yet sinners, Christ died for us.

—Rom. 5:8 KJV

For when we were yet without strength, in due time Christ died for the ungodly.

—Rom. 5:6 KJV

Herein is love, not that we loved God, but he loved us, and sent his Son to be the propitiation [appeasement] for our sins.

—1 John 4:10 KJV

When God gives us grace (what we don't deserve), the result is peace.

Therefore being justified by faith, we have peace with God.

—Rom. 5:1

While we deserved God's wrath and judgment, God gave us grace. That is absolutely and in every imaginable way counterintuitive to religion. It is also contradictory to what someone would expect from anyone they are fighting against.

The author of this letter had experienced that in a life-changing way. Grace changed Paul's story. By the grace of God, the man whose identity was wrapped up in his Jewishness became the apostle to the Gentiles; the persecutor became a preacher; and the legalistic Pharisee became the great proclaimer of the grace of God. Grace can turn the greatest nemesis of the gospel into the greatest advocate of the gospel.

The grace of God in Paul's life literally changed history. It also changes history in our lives before God because it affects the way we live on this side of heaven. Most likely, none of us of us will shape history as Paul did, but the grace of God in every redeemed, reconciled rebel changes the course of history in a marriage, a family, a neighborhood, a classroom, and a workplace.

> I'll never tire of saying that Jesus is the *agent* of our redemption, the *object* of our trust and hope, and the *repository* of all that is ours as believers.

Everything that is ours in a relationship with God, including our new and true identity, is ours in Jesus. We live between the already of the cross and the not yet of heaven by faith. That means we live as though we are totally identified with Jesus—as though we really are in Christ. We're to allow the way we think about our circumstances to be shaped by the truth that we are in Christ. We process our attitudes and the things we say and the way we act by the truth that we are in Christ.

chapter three

i am blessed – i am chosen –
i am holy – i am blameless

So far, we have learned that the Bible has the answer to the question "Who am I?" It's interesting that conventional wisdom of culture says that the brokenness of humanity is due to a lack of education and scientific advancement. But here we are with the greatest technology and the highest level of education in history, and people are only better at being bad. Instead of fighting each other face to face with sticks and stones, we can hide in bunkers and fight with drones and laser-guided bombs. Biological and scientific advances in medicine are used to create biological weapons of mass destruction. The brokenness of humanity lies far deeper than education, technology, and social theories.

Paul literally went to war against Jesus and against anyone who sought to live for and tell others about Jesus. Resist and reject were the default responses of fallen mankind to the gospel because that message and the lives of those transformed by Jesus Christ exposed the truth about ourselves that we are deeply and tragically invested in identities that are empty.

Let's look at the first part of Ephesians 1:3: "Blessed be the God and Father of our Lord Jesus Christ." "Blessed be"—that little phrase should be circled in our Bibles; it is what we call *doxology*. We could read this as "Let the God and Father of our Lord Jesus Christ be well spoken of, be eulogized." In the Old Testament, we find the psalmist David saying the same thing: "Bless the Lord, O my soul" (Ps. 103:1). David was speaking to himself. He was exhorting himself to speak well of God.

In Ephesians 1:3–14, Paul gives us the Mount Everest of theology. Kenneth Wuest says this about these verses:

> The contents of verses 3–14 make one long sentence, possibly the longest sentence of connected discourse in existence. Here we have some of the most important doctrinal words and profoundest and richest truths regarding what God has done for the saints in all the Pauline writings.

That Mount Everest of theology is the foundation, the wellspring of our doxology. Everything in this one, long sentence tells us why we should speak well of God with our words—why God is worthy of our lives being poured out to Him as a living sacrifice of praise. The point of theology is not the accumulation of biblical information. The point of theology is doxology.

> *Blessed be the God and Father of our Lord Jesus Christ, who has blessed us in Christ with every spiritual blessing in the heavenly places.*
>
> —Eph. 1:3

We bless God (speak well of God) with our words in response to how God has blessed us and done well to us and for us. You see, God has in a very tangible, eternity-shaping way blessed us with all spiritual blessings. They're called spiritual blessings because they come to us by way of the Holy Spirit. "Every spiritual blessing in the heavenly places" tells us those blessings have their origins in heaven. They come from the very throne of God by way of the Holy Spirit.

There was a lot of wealth in Ephesus. It was considered the banking center of Asia Minor and a major financial center in the Roman Empire. The Holy Spirit inspired Paul to describe everything God has done for the believer and everything God has for the believer in terms the Ephesians understood—the language of wealth, commerce, and banking.

Ephesians 1:7–8 – "according to the riches of his grace, which he lavished upon us"

Ephesians 1:18 – "what are the riches of his glorious inheritance in the saints"

Ephesians 2:7 – "so that in the coming ages he might show the immeasurable riches of his grace in kindness toward us in Christ Jesus"

Ephesians 3:8 – "To me, though I am the very least of all the saints, this grace was given, to preach to the Gentiles the unsearchable riches of Christ."

It's such a bummer when you think you have money in your checking account, but in a very awkward moment, you discover that you weren't as rich as you thought. But there's something worse than that: having wealth but not knowing you have it, or having wealth but never being able to appropriate it.

With a single word, Paul unpacks another radical, life-changing, identity-changing outcome of our rescue—*blessed.*

25

Virtually everywhere in our culture people use the word *blessed* relative to certain achievements, accomplishments or gains. *Oh, I'm so blessed.* But we need to understand that our investment portfolio, our bank accounts, where we live, our looks, or our accomplishments cannot be the sole criteria for being blessed. If those things are the only reasons we are blessed, that means the person whose stock portfolio evaporated, has nothing in the bank, lives in a ghetto, is unattractive, or has never accomplished anything of note is the opposite of blessed.

Look at this moment shortly after God created the first two human beings.

> *So God created man in his own image, in the image of*
> *God he created him; male and female he created them.*
> *And God blessed them.*
> —Gen. 1:27–28

These two people had done nothing to earn or deserve being *blessed*. God had just created them. God *blessed* them because it was always in His heart for them to be *blessed*, loved, and defined by the unmerited love of their Creator God.

Blessed means that God actively loved Adam and Eve. That was their identity.

In Jesus, you I and have the same identity as Adam and Eve when they were created to be the objects of unmerited blessing. In Jesus I am blessed. I didn't deserve to be blessed by God, but God actively did something to bless me. He actively and deliberately moved throughout human history to rescue me from every false identity and every shallow, empty identity that could never give me life and meaning. God did something. He came in human flesh to destroy sin and death so we might be brought back to the identity God intended us to have in the very beginning. I am rescued! That transforms who I am on every level.

Fallen culture tells me that my identity hinges on my performance. I always have to work for my identity—I have to earn favor. But my true identity is this: in Jesus I am the object of God's favor, and being blessed by God has nothing to do with how well I perform. The Holy Spirit goes out of His way to let us know we are the objects of God's unmerited favor as a result of being in Christ. Paul mentions Jesus 14 times in the first 14 verses of Ephesians.

The fact that I've been rescued through the cross and resurrection of Jesus doesn't mean I'm beyond failure or impervious to harm. But it does mean that no circumstance can separate me from His love that was set in action toward me and for me. To be blessed does not mean God is going to shield me from poverty or pain. God is infinitely more concerned with my eternal well-being than my temporal comfort. So who I am in Jesus guarantees me that my heavenly Father will provide me with every blessing of the Holy Spirit necessary for life between the *already* of the cross and resurrection of Jesus and the *not yet* of forever in the presence of God.

I am blessed in Christ with every spiritual blessing in the heavenly places. That's who I am; that's who you are through faith in Jesus Christ. Christian, would you say this with me?

I . . . am . . . blessed.

> *Even as he chose us in him before the foundation of the world.*
>
> —Eph. 1:4

I am chosen!

This element of our new and true identity throws us into the deep end. First, Paul tells us by inspiration of the Holy Spirit that salvation begins with God, not with humans. I didn't choose God; God chose me. The theological nomenclature is election. People have been baffled by how God can sovereignly choose us without violating our free will. Christians have debated the subject for centuries. Some Christians have thrown down the gauntlet with each other over the subject of the sovereign election of God as opposed to human responsibility.

A seminary professor once told Warren Wiersbe, "Try to explain election and you may lose your mind. But try to explain it away and you may lose your soul!"[5]

The mystery of sovereign election and human responsibility will never be solved in this life. Both sovereign election and human responsibility are taught in the Bible (John 6:37). Both are true, and both are essential. One thing is absolutely clear. Salvation begins with God, not with humans. The night before Jesus died, He said, "You have not chosen me, but I have chosen you" (John 15:16 KJV).

Second, God chose us before He created the universe. That means our salvation has nothing to do with what we have done to deserve it.

Third, God chose us . . . *in Christ.* In a fallen culture, we are desperate to earn mankind's approval. Our sense of value and worth hinges on being chosen—being accepted. Growing up, I was devastated not to be picked first for a team. Others were devastated to not be picked at all. Later as a coach, I hated cutting players. Posting the cut list made me sick. But Paul tells us that in Jesus I'm chosen by God.

Fourth, language scholars say the word translated *chosen* was used not just for the act of choosing but for being chosen for

---

5. Warren W. Wiersbe, *The Bible Exposition Commentary, Volume 2* (Wheaton, IL: Victor Books, 1996), 11.

a purpose. I am chosen for a purpose—to be holy and without blame before Him in love.

The reason He chose us is so we would be set apart to Him and for Him. That points us back to our identity as saints. Our redemption restores us to our original identity.

> *Even as he chose us in him before the foundation of the world, that we should be holy and blameless before him. In love . . .*
>
> —Eph. 1:4

This is staggering! I stand blameless before the searching, penetrating eyes of the true and living God who is beyond comprehension. I am holy—not because I'm flawless but because of the sinless life, sacrificial death, and bodily resurrection of Jesus. *That* is my new identity.

There are countless men and women who are crushed by the weight of guilt and shame—guilt for things they have done and shame for what's been done to them. Whether you sin or are sinned against, you are defiled by sin. And without the gospel, men and women are defined by the sin they've committed such as lies, sexual sin, theft, hatred, gossip, and more. Without the gospel, men and women are defined by the way they've been sinned against. What about the person who was abused as a child or raped as an adult? What about the person who has been beaten, betrayed, or abandoned? What about the person who's been stolen from, lied to, cheated on? Their lives have been polluted, made filthy, and defiled. That very real sense of being defiled by sin is at the core of incredible fear, the fear that you can never be loved or accepted, and it shapes the way you view the world and the choices you make. I'm damaged goods, you say, and that is what I deserve and the best anyone like me can hope for.

What is a man or woman to do whose lives are defined by the wrongs they've done or the ways they've been wronged? What are they to do with all their sin and all their shame? The gospel declares that on the cross, Jesus bore all our sin and all our guilt.

The Lord has laid on him the iniquity of us all.
—Isa. 53:6

On the cross Jesus bore all your shame. The gospel says that because of Jesus, you are no longer defined by the wrongs you've done or the ways you have been wronged. The gospel sets us free from all of that. Right here in Ephesians 1:4, Paul tells us that we are defined by what Jesus has done for us. Because of Jesus, because I am in Jesus, I am chosen. I am set apart to God and for God. I am without blame and without shame in the presence of God. How utterly amazing is that! But Paul doesn't stop there! In Jesus I am loved.

We need love like we need air and water. We can't live
without it.
—Timothy Keller

We can't live without love just as a fish can't live without water. In the same way fish were made to live in water, humans were made to live in the love of God. But here's the human dilemma: sin separates people from God, who is love. Ever since Genesis 3, humans have been like fish on dry ground that are dying for lack of oxygen. People are longing for a love that is not natural to them.

Love, as fallen mankind defines it, is conditional. We give love as long as we're getting love. We receive love as long as we give love, and all of that gets twisted in so many ways. Be sure to remember who wrote these things in Ephesians. Paul had blood on his hands. He found his identity in hunting down, beating, imprisoning, and even murdering men and women who loved Jesus. He was in charge of the execution of the first martyr in the history of the church (Acts 7:58). He then said that he (and every Christian) now stands without blemish—fully known and fully loved—before the searching, penetrating eyes of the true and living God. That love transcends anything humans know or can give.

> *See what kind of love the Gather has given to us, that we should be called children of God; and so we are. . . . Beloved, we are God's children now.*
>
> —1 John 3:1–2

We must always process our thoughts and emotions and circumstances in light of Jesus.

Who are you? Christian, would you say this with me?

I . . . am . . . chosen!
I . . . am . . . holy!
I . . . am . . . without blame!
I . . . am . . . loved!

chapter four

i am adopted – i am accepted

The night before Jesus died, He gave His followers a promise that would be essential to the life of any and every man or woman who follow Him.

> *These things I have spoken to you while I am still with you. But the Helper, the Holy Spirit, whom the Father will send in my name, he will teach you all things and bring to your remembrance all that I have said to you.*
> —John 14:25–26

The Christian life is all about Jesus. The Christian life is one that begins with faith in Jesus and is lived out by faith in Jesus. The Apostle Paul put it like this:

> *I live in this earthly body by trusting in the Son of God, who loved me and gave himself for me.*
> —Gal. 2:20 NLT

The Holy Spirit's passion is to reveal Jesus to us. It's His passion to shine into the hearts of men and women the light of the knowledge of the glory of God in the face of Jesus (2 Cor. 4:6). He wants us to see who Jesus is and know what Jesus did so we will love and worship Jesus. He inspired Matthew, Mark, Luke, and John to record the historical events and details of the virgin birth, the sinless life, the sacrificial death, and the bodily resurrection of Jesus.

As we move through these amazing chapters, remember that the ultimate end of our new destiny and our new identity is the worship of Jesus.

Blessed be the God and Father of our Lord Jesus Christ.
—Eph. 1:3

The Mount Everest of theology in the first three chapters of Ephesians is the foundation, the wellspring of worship. Everything in the first 14 verses of Chapter 1 tells us why God is worthy of our lives being poured out to Him as a living sacrifice of praise.

Here are the elements of our new and true identity that we've covered so far:

Verse 1 – We're given the first and perhaps the most important element of our new and true identity—I am "in Christ Jesus." The moment you believe with your heart on the Lord Jesus Christ, you are placed *into* Jesus. "In Christ" is one of the most significant outcomes of the sinless life, sacrificial death, and bodily resurrection of Jesus because every element of our relationship to God in the first three chapters is secured and experienced because we are identified with Jesus.

Verse 1 – I'm told that I am a saint. I am set apart to God and for God. That is exactly the original identity of mankind. People were made by God for God's purposes and for God's glory. Jesus lived a sinless life, died a sacrificial death, and then rose from the grave to redeem us back to that original identity.

Verse 3 – I'm told that I am blessed. That was the original identity of mankind. God made humans, and before they did a single thing to deserve it, God blessed them. Fallen culture tells me that I always have to work for my identity—I have to earn favor. But because of Jesus, I am the object of God's active love. In Jesus I am blessed. I don't deserve to be blessed by God, but God actively did something to bless me. God actively and deliberately moved in and through human history to rescue us from every false identity that could only and always fail to give us life and meaning. God did something. He came in human flesh to destroy sin and death so we might be brought back to the identity God intended us to have in the very beginning.

Verse 4 – I'm told that I am chosen. In a fallen culture, our sense of value and worth hinges on being chosen—being accepted. We are desperately at work to earn and preserve the status of being chosen by our peer group. Paul tells us that in Jesus, we're chosen by God, and it has nothing to do with what we have done to deserve it. But this element of our identity is more than just a matter of being chosen. We are chosen for a purpose.

We are chosen in Jesus to be holy. This element of our identity is tied to our identity as saints. Again, Jesus came to restore us to our original identity.

We are chosen in Jesus to be without blame. The gospel declares that because of Jesus we are no longer defined by the wrongs we've done. We are no longer defined by the ways we have been wronged. The gospel sets us free from all of that.

Verse 4 – This verse ends with the phrase "in love." Because of Jesus, I am loved. Because of Jesus, I am standing before God In love. That is my identity in Jesus. That is your identity in Jesus. We must always process our thoughts, emotions, and circumstances in light of our new identity in Jesus. In the last phrase of verse 4, the Holy Spirit takes us deeper into who we are in, through, with, and by Jesus and how that new identity connects to every circumstance of life between the already and the not yet.

In love he predestined us for adoption to himself as sons through Jesus Christ, according to the purpose of his will, to the praise of his glorious grace, with which he has blessed us in the Beloved.

—Eph. 1:4–6

God did something. He predestined us for adoption. All of us have some thoughts about adoption. Some are or know adopted children. Some are parents who adopted children. Some are in the process of adopting. The Holy Spirit inspired Paul to explain that the outcome of our rescue is a new identity in terms of adoption. It is an idea that is incredibly deep and so rich, so layered, and so nuanced that we don't want to sprint through it.

First, let's tackle the word *predestined*. Predestination and election are scary words to some and fighting words for others. Warren Wiersbe is really helpful here.

[Predestination], as it is used in the Bible, refers primarily to what God does for saved people. . . . Election seems to refer to people, while predestination refers to purposes. . . . God has predestined our adoption (Ephesians 1:5), and our conformity to Christ (Romans 8:29–30), as well as our future inheritance (Ephesians 1:11). [6]

6. Warren W. Wiersbe, *The Bible Exposition Commentary, Volume 2* (Wheaton, IL: Victor Books, 1996), 11.

The word *predestined* means "to mark out boundaries in advance." So God had a purpose. He desired to adopt us (we'll get to the "why" of that). So He marked out the boundaries in advance to make us His adopted children.

I'll personalize my experience of God adopting me. I look back at how I came to know Jesus, and I think, *Wow, God, you had that set up, didn't you?* Looking back, I saw in the moments, days, and relationships of my life how God had marked out the boundaries and the path that brought me to the exact place and moment when I would give my life to Jesus. The thing that is beyond human comprehension is that not one step along the way did I ever feel I had no control in it. It's just unsearchable how God can let us be responsible for our moral choices, responsible before Him in our choices concerning Him, and yet plan out and set up beforehand the way we would find Him and the way we would come to know Him.

This is so huge! It was God's plan and pleasure to adopt us.

A lot of men and women miss out on God's divine pleasure to adopt them because they get hung up on predestination. It was God's plan *and* God's pleasure to adopt you. Rest in that. Live in that. I pray that you are and will continue to be utterly undone by the Father's love for you, utterly undone because it was His plan and His pleasure to adopt you.

We were made to be children of God. Ever since Genesis 3 we have been orphaned. Our sin and rebellion separated us from God and left us orphaned. Fallen mankind's relationship with God can only be defined in terms of Creator and created. For God to be your Creator is one thing; for God to be your father is another. There is a deep yearning in people to get back into the arms of their Father. That explains the countless man-made religious systems. They all pretend to tell you the way to God, but they essentially say you can only know Him as Creator, and you can be His servant and His follower. Only the gospel claims that your Creator can become your Father. Only the gospel promises that because of who Jesus is and what Jesus has done can you be restored to the status of a child.

The word *adoption* tells us that sin has robbed us of our original identity as the children of God. Because of sin we are not children of God by nature. We aren't born into this world as the children of God. To become someone's child by adoption is not something that happens naturally. Adoption requires more than nature, more than biology. Adoption requires a choice. Adoption requires legal activity. That is the radical claim of the gospel. God made the choice to adopt men and women who were orphaned by sin. The cross of Jesus is the legal action. Through Christ, at Christ's expense, through the redemption that is in His blood (Eph. 1:7), we can be adopted.

By inspiration of the Holy Spirit, Paul is telling us the incredible elements of who we are because of Jesus, and this is perhaps the most amazing outcome of our rescue. Timothy Keller gave a brilliant illustration that I'll paraphrase here. Imagine a man strapped to the electric chair. He's there because he committed premeditated murder. At the last minute, the governor calls and says, "I pardon you." But what makes it more amazing is that the man was facing the electric chair because he had murdered the governor's son. But as amazing and incomprehensible as that might sound, it would be an all together different thing for that governor to adopt that man into his family, give him his own name, make him an heir of all his wealth, bring him into his home, and sit at the same table with him just as he would have with his own son.[7]

That hypothetical adoption would create a radical, revolutionary change of identity and change of status for the man in the electric chair.

Infinitely more so, being adopted by God is an unthinkably radical and revolutionary change of our identity and status. The night before Jesus died, He was talking with His Father. That prayer is called the High Priestly Prayer of Jesus (John 17). In that prayer He said to the Father, "You . . . loved them even as you loved me" (John 17:23). That is how God the Father loves anyone and everyone who has believed with their heart on the Lord Jesus Christ.

Some people are unsettled by the fact that the Bible uses the terms "sons" and "sonship" and not gender-inclusive language when it speaks of adoption. In other places Paul says that all Christians are adopted as God's sons (Rom. 8:15, 23, Gal. 4:5). That isn't sexist. In fact, it elevated the identity of Christian women beyond anything they had ever imagined. In the Roman Empire in the first century AD, only sons could be heirs. Only sons could inherit their father's property. When Paul says Christians have all been adopted as sons, he's saying that both men and women are loved by the Father, just as the Father loves Jesus. I . . . am . . . adopted. That has radical, right-here-right-now implications.

1. *Intimacy and access* – Imagine life in a time and place of an absolute monarchy. There's a horrible storm with

7. Timothy Keller, "Timothy Keller Sermon Archive, 1989-2017," *Redeemer Presbyterian Church*, accessed February 25, 2022, https://www.logos.com/product/207157/timothy-keller-sermon-archive-1989-2017. Salvation from the Outside June 14, 1992

deafening thunder and lightning striking everywhere. No commoner could run into the king's bedroom and climb into his arms to find comfort. But the children of the king can climb into the king's arms anytime for any reason.

Remember, every element of our new identity connects with everyday life between the already and the not yet. When you're desperate or when things look bleak, do you take refuge in the fact that you are loved by God the Father in the same way He loves Jesus? Do you run into the arms of the King of the universe who is your Father? Do you judge your circumstances in light of the adopting love of God, or do you let your circumstances judge God's love?

2. *Security* – We are secure in God's love because He's not just our King; He's not just our boss; He's our Father.

3. *Discipline* – Loving dads discipline their children.

    For the Lord disciplines the one he loves, and chastises every son whom he receives. It is for discipline that you have to endure. God is treating you as sons. For what son is there whom his father does not discipline? If you are left without discipline, in which all have participated, then you are illegitimate children and not sons. Besides this, we have had earthly fathers who disciplined us and we respected them. Shall we not much more be subject to the Father of spirits and live? For they disciplined us for a short time as it seemed best to them, but he disciplines us for our good, that we may share his holiness. For the moment all discipline seems painful rather than pleasant, but later it yields

*the peaceful fruit of righteousness to those who have
been trained by it.*

—Heb. 12:6–11

Everyone experiences suffering. Why? Because we live in a
broken world. But our Father is in charge of the universe. The bad
things that happen are under the control of the One who planned
and took great pleasure to adopt us. Those bad things are part
of His way of showing us how to grow up into the fullness and
likeness of our Big Brother, Jesus Christ.

Again, do you judge your circumstances in light of the
adopting love of God, or do you judge God's love in light of your
circumstances?

4. *Inheritance* – In ancient times, the idea of adoption carried the weight of giving the full rights of adulthood. To
   be adopted by God means you have the right and access
   to the riches of God's grace right here and right now. The
   man or woman who is born again into the family of God
   can immediately begin to claim their inheritance in Jesus.
   Today and as long as you live between the already and the
   not yet, you can immediately dive into and appropriate all
   the spiritual blessings you've been blessed with in Jesus.
   That is why you can meet relatively new Christians who
   are far more mature than those who have been Christians
   for a much longer period of time.

There's a trajectory to our here and now adoption. I can't come
close to getting my head around what Jesus meant when He said
the meek will inherit the earth (Matt. 5:5). It's even harder for me
to get my head around the identity of Christians being joint heirs
with Christ (Rom. 8:17). We can never in any way share in the

essential deity of Jesus or share in His essential sovereignty. But we are going to share with Him in everything else.

Let's dive into the deepest water for a moment. If you adopt a child, you can give that child everything, but you can't give them your DNA. But the Bible tells us that our heavenly Father does.

> *For I consider that the sufferings of this present time are not worth comparing with the glory that is to be revealed to us. For the creation waits with eager longing for the revealing of the sons of God. For the creation was subjected to futility, not willingly, but because of him who subjected it, in hope that the creation itself will be set free from its bondage to corruption and obtain the freedom of the glory of the children of God. For we know that the whole creation has been groaning together in the pains of childbirth until now. And not only the creation, but we ourselves, who have the firstfruits of the Spirit, groan inwardly as we wait eagerly for adoption as sons, the redemption of our bodies. For in this hope we were saved.*
>
> —Rom. 8:18–24

If we already have something, we don't have to hope for it. There's a day the universe is longing for. Right now the mountains, the hills, the oceans, every plant, every creature, every galaxy are sitting on the edge of their seats anxiously waiting and longing for the moment of our revelation as the glorious sons and daughters of the King. The universe is longing for our liberation as children of God, longing for the moment when we will finally look just like our heavenly Father, and longing for the moment when all the decay and all the flaws will be gone.

That is the trajectory of our adoption, and it should shape the way we think and live here. It gives us perspective on this side of the not yet.

> *For I consider that the sufferings of this present time are not worth comparing with the glory that is to be revealed to us.*
>
> —Rom. 8:18

> *But if we look forward to something we don't yet have, we must wait patiently and confidently.*
>
> —Rom. 8:25 NLT

God the Father loves us and predestined us to be His adopted children. It was His plan, His purpose, and His pleasure to adopt us and love us just as He loves Jesus. That love changes everything. That love—the Father's love for His children—shapes the way we view life.

Life is no longer our time and God's time or our money and God's money. It all belongs to God, and it is all laid at the Father's feet for His good pleasure. The Father didn't *tithe* His Son. Jesus didn't *tithe* His blood.

When our identity is rooted in the predestining, adopting love of God, when we begin to comprehend and experience that love, we are no longer at the center of our world. We are no longer defined by our possessions and passions. The love of the Father lays claim to our lives, and we actually begin to live as though we belong to someone greater than us.

Our lives are so defined by the love of the Father that we want to dedicate our hands, our hearts, and our homes to our Father and our Father's work and to loving His other children. Scottish evangelist Harry Drummond (1851-1897) said, "The greatest

43

thing a man can do for his Heavenly Father is to be kind to some of his other children."[8]

Paul devotes the second section of his letter to the Ephesians to telling us what that kind of life looks like.

Let's review what we've learned so far. It was God's plan and God's pleasure to make us His children. He loved us so much that He was willing to let His only Son be orphaned on the cross so we might become the adopted sons and daughters of God and experience that love. It is the Holy Spirit's job is to show us we are His children.

> *For you did not receive the spirit of slavery to fall back into fear, but you have received the Spirit of adoption as sons, by whom we cry, "Abba! Father!" The Spirit himself bears witness with our spirit that we are children of God.*
>
> —Rom. 8:15–16

> *And because you are sons, God has sent the Spirit of his Son into our hearts, crying, "Abba! Father!"*
>
> —Gal. 4:6

If you and I have any fears or anxieties, it's because we're not listening to the Spirit who tells us who we are.

HOW CAN WE KNOW if we are an adopted child of God? The answer is in Ephesians 1:6.

---

8. "Henry Drummond on Kindness," *Christian Quotes*, accessed February 25, 2022, http://christian-quotes.ochristian.com/christian-quotes_ochristian.cgi?find=Christian-quotes-by-Henry+Drummond-on-Kindness.

In love he predestined us for adoption to himself as sons through Jesus Christ, according to the purpose of his will, to the praise of his glorious grace, with which he has blessed us in the Beloved.

Three times in the first chapter we see the believer's new and true identity connected to the praise of God's glory or glorious grace. We'll see it again in verses 12 and 14. You don't just believe with your head that the grace of God is the source of your true identity. Grace is glorious to you. God's grace captures your heart and your imagination. You praise God for it. You adore God for it.

I . . . am . . . adopted.

chapter five

i am redeemed – i am forgiven

Ephesians 1:7

The Hebrew title for Genesis, the first book of the Bible, is "Beginning," taken from the opening words of the book: "In the beginning." It doesn't begin with a thesis defending or explaining the existence and nature of God. It just launches with the declaration, "In the beginning, God." It opens with a declaration of God's existence, and then says, "In the beginning, God created." Before anything ever was, there was God. He created the material universe out of nothing—*ex nihilo*, the Latin phrase that means "out of nothing."

We're told that God completed His creative work by creating a man and then a woman. It is there in the first two chapters of the opening book of the Bible that we find the original version of a man and a woman. It's right there that we find the answer to the question "Who am I?" because it's there that we're told that a person's identity—their deepest sense of meaning—was completely wrapped up in their relationship to God. Humans bore and reflected the image and glory of God to live for the glory of

God. They were made to live in and live from that original identity. We don't know how long they lived in and from that identity, but in Genesis 3 we're told that our first parents sought to establish an identity that was rooted in their independence from God and the pursuit of their own glory. We can't even begin to fathom the eternal consequences of that decision, and every day we learn more and more about the scope of the temporal consequences of that decision. Everything that is broken about this world is traced back to this crisis of identity.

In the face of that incredible betrayal we are stunned by what was in the heart of God for the ones who betrayed Him. The gospel tells us that the Rejected One came to rescue the ones who rejected Him. He came to rescue us from the eternal consequences of our sin and rebellion and restore us to fellowship with God—restore us to our original and true identity.

Let's take some time to review and look again at what's in the first verses of Ephesians 1. The book of Ephesians is perhaps the most majestic expression and explanation of all God has done for us in, through, with, and by Jesus. We've discovered who we are *because of* Jesus, who we are *in* Jesus, who we are *with* Jesus, who we are *through* Jesus, and who we are *by* Jesus.

Verse 1 – First and foremost, we are *in Christ Jesus*. Our identity is wrapped up in His identity. Every element of our new and true identity is tethered to that outcome of our rescue.

Verse 1 – In Jesus we are *saints*, set apart to God and for God (that was mankind's original identity).

Verse 3 – In Jesus we are *blessed* "with every spiritual blessing in the heavenly places" (that was mankind's original identity; we were made to be the object of God's active love).

Verse 4 – In Jesus we are *chosen* for a purpose. He chose us so we would be *holy*, set apart to Him and for Him. Again, Jesus came to restore us to our original identity.

We are chosen so we will be blameless before Him. Jesus the blameless one bore our sin and our shame. The identity of every believer is immersed in the identity of the blameless one. We're no longer defined by the wrongs we've done. We're no longer defined by the ways we've been wronged. The gospel sets us free from all that.

Verse 4 – In Jesus we are *loved*. That is our identity in Jesus. We've learned that our sin has left us orphaned. For God to be your Creator is one thing; for God to be your Father is another. The gospel tells us that God wanted to rescue us and take us back to our original identity as His children.

Verse 5 – It was God's plan, *purpose*, and pleasure to adopt us and love us just as He loves Jesus. Here's something Charles Spurgeon said about our adoption:

> A man, when he adopts a child, sometimes is moved thereto by its extraordinary beauty, or at other times by its intelligent manners and winning disposition. But, beloved, when God passed by the field in which we were lying . . . he found a rebellious child, a filthy, frightful, ugly child; he took it to his bosom, and said, "Black though thou art, thou art comely in my eyes through my son Jesus; unworthy though thou art, yet I cover thee with his robe, and in thy brother's garments I accept thee;" and taking us, all unholy and unclean, just as we were, he took us to be his — his children, his for ever.[9]

That love changes everything. First, Paul tells us that the life of every adopted rebel results in the praise of God. "To the praise

---

9. Charles H. Spurgeon, *Spurgeon's Sermons, Volume 7* (Albany, OR: Ages Software, 1998).

of his glorious grace, with which he has blessed us in the Beloved" (Eph. 1:6).

Think about this: the new heaven and the new earth are going to be populated with adopted rebels. Throughout eternity, no matter where we are in His forever Kingdom, we are going to look at one another and say, "Lord! You are so worthy of praise! That person was a rebel, just like me. They deserved your wrath, just like I deserved your wrath. Your grace is so glorious that you not only adopted me, but you adopted them."

On this side of forever we deserve to live as orphans in a fallen world. But God's glorious grace has changed all that. Paul Tripp, said, "You're not just anybody, because God has shed his love on you, adopted you into his family and named you one of his children.

Right here, right now you are God's adopted child. You are loved just as He loves Jesus. That love makes every adopted rebel a worshiper. We want to pour out our lives as a living sacrifice of praise for His glorious grace. That love shapes the way we live in the here and now. When our identity is rooted in the predestined, adopting love of God, when we begin to comprehend and experience that love, we are no longer at the center of our world. We are no longer defined by our possessions and passions.

The love of the Father lays claim to our lives and makes us live like we belong to someone greater than ourselves. Our lives are so defined by the love of the Father that we want to dedicate our hands, our hearts, and our homes to our Father and our Father's work and to loving His other children. And that results in the praise of His glorious grace. The world around you is provoked to think about how glorious and gracious your God must be to cause you to live in such a way.

I . . . am . . . in Jesus.

I . . . am . . . a saint.

I . . . am . . . blessed.

I . . . am . . . chosen.

I . . . am . . . holy.

I . . . am . . . without blame.

I . . . am . . . loved.

I . . . am . . . adopted.

I don't want to leave verse 6 without looking at the way it reads in the King James Version.

> *To the praise of the glory of his grace, wherein he hath made us accepted in the beloved.*
>
> —Eph. 1:6 KJV

Every replacement identity is to the end that we will be accepted. Insult is rough. Failure is hard to take. But rejection is a wound that can't be described. Here's the deal. We deserve to be rejected by God. We can never make ourselves acceptable to God. But by His grace—God doing for us what we do not deserve and could never earn—God has made us accepted in Christ.

That is my forever identity. It will never change. Here's what happened so we could have that forever identity. Jesus took every ounce of rejection that you and I deserve so we would never again see the back of God's head.

Who am I? Who are you? Christian, would you say this with me?

I . . . am . . . accepted.

> *In him we have redemption through his blood, the forgiveness of our trespasses, according to the riches of his grace, which he lavished upon us.*
>
> —Eph. 1:7–8

In Jesus, I am *redeemed*. This element of our identity is so incredibly important. The word *redemption* means "the act of purchasing and setting free by paying a price." There were 60 million slaves in the Roman Empire. Humans were bought and sold like pieces of furniture. But someone could purchase a slave and set them free. The idea of a ransom defines the reality of someone's life. You only pay a ransom if somebody is in slavery, if they're in some sort of bondage, or if they've been captured or are in prison.

If we are ever going to be restored to our true identity, we need to embrace everything it implies about us. It's one thing to see that you're broken and need help. But it is a different thing all together to know that you're a slave and you're in bondage and can't buy your way out. From Genesis 1:1 to Revelation 22:21, the Bible is very clear about the condition of mankind. He doesn't just need a little help or a little life coaching. He doesn't just need to find the thing that best lends meaning to life and then fine-tune that identity. The Bible says that every man and woman is fallen. Every man and woman is in captivity. The Bible says that you and I are beyond being helped. We don't need a helper; we need a Redeemer.

Fallen mankind doesn't like that message at all. That's why men and women are okay with religion and going to church. They think church is there to fix their lives, sharpen their replacement identity, and help them have the life they want to have. How prevalent is that view? People have purchased millions of copies of books about your best life now or how to be a better you. They are happy to check out religion if that's what religion will deliver. They're happy to go to church if that's what they're going to hear.

Maybe some of you have brought friends with you to church, and afterward they say something like this: "I like some of the things the preacher had to say, but man, that guy was too heavy. I mean, I'm willing to admit I'm flawed, and I'll even use the word *sin*, but that guy made it sound like I'm in dire straits without Jesus."

For the Bible to use the word *ransom* and refer to Jesus as Redeemer says that we are in dire straits. We are in bondage, we are in slavery, and we're under the sentence of death. The word *ransom* means that a tremendous price was paid. Something of tremendous value was paid so we could be set free. The fact that a ransom had to be paid for us tells us that we are utterly incapable of paying the price. That's another thing people don't want to hear. They don't want to be told that they are so enslaved, so held under the power and penalty of sin, that they can't buy their own freedom. They don't want to be told that their sin is so bad that Jesus *had* to die, that there's no other way they can be saved.

The Bible says we were in bondage to sin, the slaves of sin. We were slaves to the replacement identities we had looked to and trusted in to give us life. We were in prison with the death penalty, "for the wages of sin is death" (Rom. 6:23). That was our condition. But the gospel declares that in Him (Jesus) we have redemption. Once again, Jesus is the agent of our redemption.

In Peter's first epistle, we're told that the purchase price for our redemption was not silver or gold or things that perish. It was the precious blood of Jesus. The last words of Jesus from the cross were "It is finished"—literally, paid in full. The blood of Jesus shed on the cross is the currency of our redemption. It is the only payment that covers our ransom.

> *Truly no man can ransom another, or give to God the price of his life, for the ransom of their life is costly and can never suffice, that he should live on forever and never see the pit.*
>
> —Ps. 49:7–9

It is the only payment God can accept, the only payment God will accept to ransom us from the penalty and power of sin. The bodily resurrection of Jesus three days after His death on the cross is the guarantee that His shed blood is sufficient to ransom us.

It is because (and only because) of the redemption that is in Jesus, the ransom price of His shed blood, that I am free from slavery to sin (Rom. 6) and free from the power of Satan and the corrupting influence of the world that is organizing itself without God and against God (Gal. 1:4, Col. 1:13–14).

Look at this scene in heaven around the throne of Jesus.

> *And they sang a new song, saying, "Worthy are you to take the scroll and to open its seals, for you were slain, and by your blood you ransomed people for God from every tribe and language and people and nation."*
>
> —Rev. 5:9

This is huge! The ransom that was paid not only defines me as redeemed, but it defines me as His purchased possession.

> *Or do you not know that your body is a temple of the Holy Spirit within you, whom you have from God? You are not your own, for you were bought with a price. So glorify God in your body.*
>
> —1 Cor. 6:19

That is at the core of the second part of Ephesians. Who we are (ransomed) determines how we live.

Who am I? Who are you? Christian, would you say this with me?

I . . . am . . . redeemed.

*In him we have . . . the forgiveness of our trespasses,
according to the riches of his grace, which he lavished
upon us.*

—Eph. 1:7–8

All of us have to admit to being haunted by regrets. We all
know the burden of carrying the weight of horrible words spoken
or kind words unspoken. We know the guilt of unloving, selfish
things we've done. We try to deal with our guilt by blame-
shifting and denial. Then there's the reality that people withhold
forgiveness or give it in part, or they say they forgive you but they
hold your past against you.

In Jesus, I am forgiven—completely and forever forgiven. It
doesn't matter what I have done or will do. Jesus died for every
sin. Because of the cross and resurrection of Jesus, God doesn't
hold your sin against you. Because of the cross and resurrection
of Jesus, God isn't going to punish you.

I hope this captures your heart with a sense of awe and
adoration for God. In Genesis, all God had to do was say "Let there
be light," and there was light. He merely spoke, and the physical
universe came into being. But God couldn't just say "Let there be
forgiveness." I say this from the puny point of view of a speck on
a speck in God's universe, and I say it with absolute reverence.
Forgiveness is so great, so problematic, that even the omnipotent
God could not just speak it into existence.

Here's why. The Bible says that God is holy. His absolute,
utter, moral perfection is essential to His very nature. The Bible
says that because God is holy, He must also be just. He must
judge sin—all sin. But the Bible also says that God is love. A lot of
people believe that because God is love, He can forgive us in the
same way He created by simply saying, "Let Richard be forgiven."
But here's the problem. God does love me. He wants to restore me

to Himself. He can't bear to see me spend forever separated from Him in hell. But how does He do that without compromising His holiness? How does He do that without compromising His justice? How can God make us right with Him without making Himself wrong?

Look at part of this psalm:

> *Mercy and truth are met together; righteousness and peace have kissed each other.*
>
> —Ps. 85:10 KJV

That is exactly what God did through the cross of Jesus.

> *For all have sinned and fall short of the glory of God, and are justified by his grace as a gift, through the redemption that is in Christ Jesus, whom God put forward as a propitiation by his blood, to be received by faith. This was to show God's righteousness, because in his divine forbearance he had passed over former sins. It was to show his righteousness at the present time, so that he might be just and the justifier of the one who has faith in Jesus.*
>
> —Rom. 3:23–26

That makes the gospel unlike any other man-made religion or philosophy. Why on earth would God ever send His Son to die on the cross if there was any other way that we could be saved? Jesus Christ being nailed to a Roman cross tells us that we matter to the only One who matters. Someone framed it like this: "Do you know what Calvary is? Do you know what it is? It's damnation, and he took it for us lovingly."

Who am I? Who are you? Christian, would you say this with me?

I . . . am . . . forgiven.

That's why Paul the apostle wrote this:

As for me, may I never boast about anything except the cross of our Lord Jesus Christ. Because of that cross, my interest in this world has been crucified, and the world's interest in me has also died.

—Gal. 6:14 NLT

I boast in the cross of Jesus because in the cross I discover how expensive it was for me to be redeemed and forgiven. If I'm really boasting in the cross—really understanding the price of forgiveness—then I'm going to come to understand how forgiveness works on the human level. Forgiving the person who has wronged me is going to be expensive. In other words, withholding forgiveness is directly associated with my failure to understand that God held nothing back in order to forgive me.

In light of what it cost God to forgive me, how can I withhold forgiveness for someone else? When someone says, "You have to forgive," my default response (depending on the offense) is often, "It's too hard!" The cross of Jesus Christ says to you and to me, "Of course it is!" If I think forgiveness is easy, I have a deficient understanding of what it cost God to forgive me.

Again, who I am (forgiven) determines how I live.

Get rid of all bitterness, rage, anger, harsh words, and slander, as well as all types of evil behavior. Instead, be kind to each other, tenderhearted, forgiving one another, just as God through Christ has forgiven you.

—Eph. 4:31–32 NLT

chapter six

there is a plan – i am in the plan – i am safe in the plan

Ephesians 1:7–12

Ephesians is a book about *who* the Christian is, *how* the Christian lives, and *how* the Christian stands. It's a Mount Everest of theology. The first 13 verses are its peak. In the original language, those verses are one long sentence with 202 words. We need that massive sentence broken into subsentences so we can understand it. If we want to figure out the point of a sentence, we need to find the subject and the verb—who the doer is and what the doer is doing. Our subsentences let us know that God is the doer, and He has done a lot for us in, through, with, and by Jesus. He's blessed us, chosen us, loved us, adopted us, and accepted us. Our identity is wrapped up in every one of those divine actions, and the love of God is what drives each of those actions. What God did defines who we are.

We've looked at how God redeemed us and forgave us in Jesus. Those words tell us what God did. But what God had to do tells us a lot about the condition of people. Redeemed is slave language.

For God to redeem us means that a person is a slave and needs to be set free. Forgiveness is legal language. For God to forgive tells us that mankind is guilty of a cosmic crime.

That doesn't fit the narrative of a fallen culture. It's safe to say that nearly everyone knows the world isn't what it should be, but the overwhelming consensus is that human beings are basically good and getting better. That's pretty much what it means to be progressive and pretty much what drives progressive culture and progressive politics. Mankind just needs a little help. But the evidence doesn't bear that out. Despite millennia of human history, and advances in education and technology, we've only gotten better at being bad. There really is such a thing as evil. Even worse than that, evil is not just out there; it's inside of me and you.

It's our fingerprints that are all over the broken world. The Bible tells us that each of us is a guilty party. We've all made contributions to the brokenness of our world. The average person who acknowledges the existence of God pretty much thinks that if there is a God, it's His job to forgive us. The idea that there really is a God and that God is just and is the judge is unacceptable. That is odd because no one wants to live in a world where there's no justice and people get away with evil. Civilized countries have laws to govern their citizens. They understand that breaking the law carries consequences. We live in God's universe. He has made us, and He's given His law for our well-being. We have all broken God's law. We are all guilty. We hate the idea that we're guilty before Him and deserve justice. David Robertson said, "Who is going to pay for our sin? The Bible says that we can – if we wish. But that is what hell is."

Our brokenness is so real, so deep, and so ingrained, and our guilt is so great before God that we need more than a helper. We need a Redeemer. We need a Savior. That is the meaning of the cross of Jesus.

Paul tells us, "In him [Jesus] we have redemption through his blood, the forgiveness of our trespasses" (Eph. 1:7). Then Paul tells us that God did all that "according to the riches of His grace, which he lavished upon us" (Eph. 1:7–8). We needed God to do for us what we don't deserve and could never earn. But God didn›t provide that grace like a prescription dose of medicine that we can only have in an exact amount per day. No, Paul says God redeemed us and forgave us according to an overdose of His grace. He poured out on us more grace than we could ever need or ever hope for, an abundance of grace that is so great that it will amaze us for all eternity.

> *So that in the coming ages he might show the immea-surable riches of his grace in kindness toward us in Christ Jesus.*
>
> —Eph. 2:7

But Paul doesn't stop there. God overdosed us with redeeming, forgiving, transforming grace in all wisdom and insight. God didn't blindly lavish His grace upon us. He knew everything about the ones he was redeeming. He knew everything about the ones He was forgiving. He knew every sin of mine and every sin of yours that He would lay upon Jesus.

God has blessed us, chosen us, loved us, adopted us, accepted us, redeemed us, and forgiven us. Again, our identity is wrapped up in every one of those divine actions, and the love of God is driving them. What God has done defines who we are.

In Ephesians 1:7–12, we come to a point in Paul's long sentence where we discover that everything God has done for us in, through, with, and by Jesus has a trajectory; it is moving toward a glorious conclusion. In other words, God has a plan, and everyone who has believed with their heart on the Lord Jesus is in His plan and safe in His plan.

In him we have redemption through his blood, the forgiveness of our trespasses, according to the riches of his grace, which he lavished upon us, in all wisdom and insight making known to us the mystery of his will, according to his purpose, which he set forth in Christ as a plan for the fullness of time, to unite all things in him, things in heaven and things on earth. In him we have obtained an inheritance, having been predestined according to the purpose of him who works all things according to the counsel of his will, so that we who were the first to hope in Christ might be to the praise of his glory.

—Eph. 1:7–12

Verse 9 says there is a plan for history, and the Christian is in the know. The Christian is an insider. It might sound weird, but here's the truth. As someone who has believed with my heart on the Lord Jesus, I can say that I am in the know. It's not because I'm some super investigative reporter. It's not because I've figured it out. The biblical concept of mystery is not the same as a mystery in literature or in a movie or TV series. In the Bible, a mystery is something unknown to people and unknowable by people unless God makes it known. That's exactly what Paul says God does for the Christian when he said God made known to us "the mystery of his will."

The mystery has to do with history. He's telling us there is a plan for history, and God has the plan for it. The world is not without opinions on how history is going to play out. By the way, the whole post-apocalyptic genre of movies is someone's eschatology in cinematic art form.

Here's one opinion. There is no plan. Bertrand Russell lived from 1872 to 1970. He was an intellectual giant. He is widely held to be one of the 20th century's premier logicians. He was also one of the most adamant atheists of the last century. Russell was once asked what he would do if he died and found himself standing before the Almighty who demanded to know why Russell did not believe in Him. Russell replied that he would look God in the eye and say, "Not enough evidence, sir!"[10] Here's the utterly bleak end of a godless universe according to Russell:

> That Man is the product of causes which had no prevision of the end they were achieving; that his origin, his growth, his hopes and fears, his loves and his beliefs, are but the outcome of accidental collocations of atoms . . . that all the labours of the ages, all the devotion, all the inspiration, all the noonday brightness of human genius, are destined to extinction in the vast death of the solar system, and that the whole temple of Man's achievement must inevitably be buried beneath the debris of a universe in ruins. . . . Only within the scaffolding of these truths, only on the firm foundation of unyielding despair, can the soul's habitation henceforth be safely built.[11]

That is the brutally honest reality of atheism, that we're here by accident. And by the way, they also say our solar system is going to die, and the universe will succumb to entropy. That means that nothing you do, nothing anybody has ever done, will ever be remembered. There is no plan. That means unyielding despair.

---

10. Andy Bannister, *The Atheist Who Didn't Exist, Google Books.*
11. Bertrand Russell, "A Free Man's Worship," December 1903, accessed February 25, 2022, https://www.academia.edu/1278006/Bertrand_Russell_A_Free_Mans_Worship.

Here's how that worldview plays out in everyday existence (I deliberately said existence, not life, because according to Russell, we are only part of a death march into oblivion). The here and now is the only thing we can look to for meaning. There can be no point to adversity or suffering or disappointment. Such stuff is salt on the wound, insult to injury. There is no ultimate reference point for good or for right or wrong, so you make decisions based on personal gratification. In the no-plan version of our world, the things you can look to for meaning are things that have no ultimate meaning. What I do, what I have, what I create, and who I know will all be buried beneath the debris of a universe in ruins.

The Bible says no, there is a plan, and God has made known to us the mystery of His will. Kenneth Wuest is really helpful here. He says there is a Greek word translated "a desire based upon the reason." But that is not the word the Holy Spirit inspired Paul to use here. Paul used the word *thelēma* (θελημα), "a desire based upon the emotions."[12] God's will or desire comes from His heart of love.

Paul tells us that the passionate plan of God, the good pleasure of God, was set forth and worked out in Jesus Christ. "Making known to us the mystery of his will, according to his purpose, which he set forth in Christ" (Eph. 1:9).

The plan is about Jesus.

Let's read and consider Ephesians 1:10 (NLT):

> *And this is the plan: At the right time he will bring everything together under the authority of Christ—everything in heaven and on earth.*

---

12. Kenneth S. Wuest, Wuest's Word Studies from the Greek New Testament for the English Reader (Grand Rapids, MI: Eerdmans, 1997).

God has a plan for the fulfillment of the ages. Absolutely everything in history is part of that plan.

> *In him we have obtained an inheritance, having been predestined according to the purpose of him who works all things according to the counsel of his will.*
>
> —Eph. 1:11

There are two very big words and one phrase here that leave a lot of people perplexed and troubled. *Predestined*—we've already looked at that word in relation to God adopting us. Predestination refers to purpose. It means to mark out boundaries in advance. The other big word is *purpose*, the word that means a blueprint—a plan. The boundaries of our lives have been marked out according to the blueprint—the plan—of Him who works all things according to the counsel of His will

Everything that happens is part of God's plan. Even Bible-believing, Jesus-loving men and women struggle with absolute power. In a fallen world, we know by experience that power tends to corrupt and that absolute power tends to corrupt absolutely. Those with power exercise their will and get their way, no matter who's in their way and at the expense of anyone in their way because all that matters is getting their way. But God is holy. *Holy* means "separate from or other than." God is separate from His creation. His power is not like human power; it is greater. His control is not like mans' control; it is greater.

Paul has gone out of his way to talk about the will of God in terms of the pleasure God has to include us in His will. It is God's pleasure to adopt us. It's what He wanted to do, and it gave Him great pleasure to do it. By inspiration of the Holy Spirit, Paul wants us to know that the God who always accomplishes His will knew every wretched, wrecked thing about us. He knew what every sin we ever committed would bring upon Jesus, and yet He still redeemed us and forgave us with an overdose of grace. That same grace has included us in God's ultimate purpose. God has included us in His plan at His expense.

So to say that everything that happens is part of God's plan immediately begs the question, are we free or is there a plan we can't escape? The answer is yes! Finite, flawed human reason has forever tried to process this question as an either-or problem. I'm either free or a pawn in an inescapable plan.

This blueprint of God Paul is talking about, the plan God is absolutely going to accomplish (we'll see what that plan is in just a bit), was going to run right through the descendants of a man named Abraham. Abraham had a son named Isaac who had a son named Jacob, who was given a new name—Israel—by God. He had 12 sons who would become the 12 tribes of the nation of Israel. By the time we get to Genesis 37, the nation through whom God was going to bring Jesus into the world was in its infancy. Counting wives and kids, the population of that nation was about 66. There was a huge famine that would pose an existential threat to the lineage of Abraham and along with it the blueprint of God's redeeming plan and purpose. God was going to work out everything according to the counsel of His will.

Along the way there would be a lot of choices made. Ten of Jacob's sons hated their brother Joseph. They got together and plotted his murder. They threw Joseph into a pit where they were going to leave him to die, but then they saw a caravan approaching, and instead of leaving Joseph to die in the pit, they sold him as a slave to the people in the caravan, who carried him to Egypt where he was sold as a slave to a guy named Potiphar. There Joseph was falsely accused of sexually assaulting Potiphar's wife and unjustly thrown into prison. Amazingly, throughout all the moral and relational chaos in the story, Joseph emerges from prison in Egypt to become the second most powerful man in Egypt under Pharaoh. Through a vision, Joseph foretells the coming seven-year famine and makes plans to survive it. And by virtue of those plans, Jacob and his sons survive the famine.

On a human level, Joseph was the victim of gross injustice. It was 10 against one. The brothers planned it all. That was the human side of the story. But we're told this in the Psalms:

> *When he summoned a famine on the land and broke*
> *all supply of bread, he had sent a man ahead of them,*
> *Joseph, who was sold as a slave.*
> —Ps. 105:16–17

Here's how Joseph explained it to his brothers after they discovered that the powerful man they had to deal with was actually their brother Joseph.

> *As for you, you meant evil against me, but God meant*
> *it for good, to bring it about that many people should*
> *be kept alive, as they are today.*
> —Gen. 50:20

That entire narrative fits Paul's language in Ephesians 1:11 about God's plan.

Boundaries marked out in advance, God's blueprint, God working all things according to the counsel of His will—there was no absence of human choice in the narrative. Ten men freely exercised their will to destroy their brother, but God worked all things according to His will.

This is no small side note in light of the real-life story of Joseph. The fact that God has an ultimate plan and that we are included in God's perfect plan means there can be meaning in suffering, meaning in disappointment, and something glorious even when we suffer injustice. The One in whom the whole plan is contained is the proof of it.

> *People of Israel, listen! God publicly endorsed Jesus the Nazarene by doing powerful miracles, wonders, and signs through him, as you well know. But God knew what would happen, and his prearranged plan was carried out when Jesus was betrayed. With the help of lawless Gentiles, you nailed him to a cross and killed him. But God released him from the horrors of death and raised him back to life, for death could not keep him in its grip.*
>
> Acts 2:22–24 NLT

Joseph's brothers plotted to put an end to Joseph, but their free choices and actions actually served the blueprint of God to save the nation of Israel from extinction. The ethnic brothers of Jesus plotted to put an end to Jesus, but their free choices and actions served the blueprint of God to redeem and forgive us by the shed blood of Jesus.

Fatalism says your choices don't matter, but against fatalism the Bible says your choices matter. There are consequences for what you do. God holds you responsible for what you're doing. No one is forcing you to do the things you're doing. You are free and responsible, and there are consequences.

At the same time, God uses all our free choices. He works through them and brings His power to bear on them so everything that is freely chosen only works according to His perfect plan. You are free, and yet absolutely there is a plan.

Let's carry this over into the passionate, loving plans and purposes of God for every believer. "For those whom he foreknew he also predestined to be conformed to the image of his Son"

(Rom. 8:29). That is God's blueprint for every Christian. We are predestined to it. You might say, *Well, wait a minute. If I'm predestined to be like Christ, then my choices don't matter. If I'm predestined, it doesn't really matter what I do.* Paul says that yes, you are predestined, and what you do does matter.

Here's the deal. We simply don't have enough information to know how God can accomplish His perfect will and never diminish people's moral responsibility. But that is exactly what the Bible tells us. We want to avoid the trap of fatalism and say, "What's the use?" And we want to avoid the trap of thinking that our place in the plan and the working out of the plan hang on our performance.

God tells us to run the race. God tells us to love Him and love others for Him and to Him. He holds us accountable for what He asks. We can and we will mess up. But here's the deal, Christians. There *is* a plan. We are *in the plan* because God has overdosed us with grace. We are *in the plan*, and we are *safe in the plan*. We might mess up, but because of Jesus, we can't ultimately mess up because in Jesus, God has more grace for us than we will ever need.

There is a plan, we are in the plan, and we are safe in the plan— and it's all moving toward Christ. God is—right now—in every moment of every life, working everything together according to his plan toward a specific end "as a plan for the fullness of time, to unite all things in him, things in heaven and things on earth" (Eph. 1:10).

The point of the whole plan of history is to bring all things in heaven and on earth together. The heavenly realm hasn't been unified since the moment Lucifer decided to exalt himself over and above the Most High God. Chaos in the spiritual realm visited our planet. The architect of that heavenly revolt came and convinced our first parents to join in that same revolt. The story of planet earth since Genesis 3 is captured in the title of a Bob Dylan song,

"Everything Is Broken." Renowned poet William Butler Yeats wrote in his poem "The Second Coming" that "things fall apart; the centre cannot hold; mere anarchy is loosed upon the world."

The second law of thermodynamics says that things tend toward disorder. The universe is running down. Everything is falling apart. That's what Bertrand Russell was talking about. The same thing is true in the spiritual realm, but the Bible explains why. When our relationship with God fell apart, every other relationship fell apart, including our ability to know ourselves. We ask the question "Who am I?" because we don't know who we are.

There is coming a point when the seasons of human history will culminate as a plan for the fullness of time, to unite all things in Him, things in heaven and things on earth. God is going to sum up everything in Jesus Christ. God is bringing everything to the place where finally Jesus Christ, the true and forever King, is ruling. It is only when Jesus Christ is King that all the things that are falling apart will come together again. Only then will all things be healed.

Fallen mankind has hoped that political, military, and social leaders would bring everything together. But fallen people can't govern themselves, let alone govern other fallen men and women. There is no resolution after millennia of human rule. It's falling apart because we've put ourselves in the place of the King. God has been working in all of history toward the moment when "at the name of Jesus every knee [shall] bow . . . and every tongue confess that Jesus Christ is Lord" (Phil. 2:10–11).

Once again, all things will be made whole under Jesus the King. The King was torn to pieces so we could be made whole. The Son of God was crushed so we could be healed.

chapter seven

i am sealed

Ephesians 1:13-14

This letter to the Christians in Ephesus opens with a very simple introduction by the author.

> *Paul, an apostle of Christ Jesus by the will of God.*
>
> —Eph. 1:1

But that's all he had to say about himself. There's not a single word recalling what he did in Ephesus, how he lived there, or what he said there. He had one compelling, majestic, massive theme that he simply couldn't contain. He was like a jet on the runway cleared for takeoff, brakes on, and engines wide open. In verse 2, he releases the brake. I know this is a different metaphor, but it's as if suddenly Mount Everest is thrust upward right before us. It's the Mount Everest of gospel truth. Paul goes from nothing to say about himself to the longest sentence in all ancient literature—202 words—that tells them about God and all God has done for them (and us) in, through, with, and by Jesus. He's blessed us, chosen us, loved us, adopted us, accepted us, redeemed us, and forgiven us. God did all that, and He did it all according to the riches of His grace that He lavished upon us.

Our identity is wrapped up in every one of those divine actions. Our fallen culture tells us that we are what we do. But by inspiration of the Holy Spirit, Paul says no! What God did defines who we are.

Paul didn't stop there. He says that everything God has done for us in, through, with, and by Jesus has a trajectory that is moving toward a glorious conclusion. God has a plan, and everyone who has believed with their heart on the Lord Jesus is *in* His plan and is *safe* in His plan. And the plan is all about Jesus.

> *Making known to us the mystery of his will, according to his purpose, which he set forth in Christ as a plan for the fullness of time, to unite all things in him, things in heaven and things on earth.*
>
> —Eph. 1:9–10

And he's still not finished! He still has more to say about what God has done in, through with, and by Jesus.

> *In him [Jesus] you also, when you heard the word of truth, the gospel of your salvation, and believed in him, were sealed with the promised Holy Spirit, who is the guarantee of our inheritance until we acquire possession of it, to the praise of his glory.*
>
> —Eph. 1:13–14

Let's not miss this: becoming a Christian doesn't start by your doing something. It starts by hearing something. What is it you hear? You hear a word, a message, a body of content. You hear truth; you hear the gospel—the good news. A lot of people want to discount the claim that the gospel is truth by saying there is no such thing as truth, that no one can say what is true and what isn't. But their objection becomes their problem. They think the absence of truth is going to free them, but it suffocates them because if there is no such thing as truth, they can't object to anything. G. K. Chesterton said it well in his book *Orthodoxy*. "By rebelling against everything he has lost his right to rebel against anything."

Man cannot live without truth. The word of truth is the gospel. The gospel is not spiritual advice. The word *gospel* means an announcement of something that has happened in history. And that sets Christianity apart from every other religious system. Religion says here's what you have to do to be saved. The gospel says here's what God has done in history to save you. You become a Christian when you hear the truth—the good news, the record of what God has done to save us in the sending of His Son Jesus—and believe in Jesus. You trust in, cling to, and rely upon Jesus to save you.

There are those who insist that believing the gospel—the record of what God has done to save us—is something they could never do. They say, "I can't believe in Christianity because of what the Bible says about sexual behavior, sexual preference, and gender." But here's where they're confused. Believing that the Bible has it wrong on sex and gender doesn't mean that Jesus never died on a cross and rose from the grave. If you tell them that, they will say, "What does the cross and resurrection of Jesus have to do with how wrong I think the Bible is when it talks about sex and gender?" The answer is—*everything*!

You can't reject Christianity because you disagree with what the Bible says about sexual preference, sexual behavior, or gender. If Jesus isn't God who became man, lived a sinless life, died on the cross for our sins, and rose from the grave, you don't have to believe anything the Bible says about sex and gender. But if Jesus is, in fact, God who became man, lived a sinless life, died on a cross for our sins, and rose bodily from the grave, then you have to deal with everything the Bible says about how to live. You don't start with what the Bible has to say about how to live to decide whether the gospel is true. You start with what the Bible claims God has done. You start with what the Bible says about Jesus. That's where Christianity begins. You become a Christian when you hear the truth of the gospel and believe in Jesus.

So how can a person know they've believed in Jesus unto salvation? "In him [Jesus] you also, when you heard the word of truth, the gospel of your salvation, and believed in him, were sealed with the promised Holy Spirit" (Eph. 1:13). The language may sound obscure to us, but it wasn't to the Ephesians. A seal authenticated and marked ownership, and it also secured an object.

Let's see how those things describe what it means to be sealed with the Holy Spirit.

A seal authenticated and marked ownership. *Authenticate* = to prove or show to be true or genuine; to validate.

Paul says that a Christian is someone who hears the truth of the gospel and believes in Jesus. He says that when they believe, the Holy Spirit seals that person—authenticates that person's faith in Jesus, shows that person that their faith is true and genuine, and validates their faith in Jesus.

Here's how the Holy Spirit does that. The moment we hear the truth of the gospel and believe in Jesus, the Holy Spirit indwells us and unites us with Jesus. There is no salvation unless the believer is united with Jesus.

John Murray wrote, "Union with Christ is the central truth of the whole doctrine of salvation."[13] John Calvin explained it this

---

13. John Murray, *Redemption Accomplished and Applied* (Grand Rapids, MI: Eerdmans, 1955), 161.

way: "How do we receive those benefits which the Father bestowed on his only-begotten Son? . . . First, we must understand that as long as Christ remains outside of us, and we are separated from him, all that he has suffered and done for the salvation of the human race remains useless and of no value for us." [14]

It is the Holy Spirit who unites us with Jesus. When we believe the gospel, the Holy Spirit places us into Christ (1 Cor. 12:13, Gal. 3:27).

"In Christ" is the language of union, the language of position. It is the language of what it means to be saved.

> *In those days you were living apart from Christ. . . .*
> *You lived in this world without God and without hope.*
> —Eph. 2:12 NLT

But the moment we believed the good news, the Holy Spirit placed us into Christ. Our union with Christ is so crucial that the Holy Spirit inspired Paul to use the phrase "in Christ" about 160 times in the 13 letters he penned. Justification, reconciliation, redemption, adoption, sanctification, resurrection life, eternal life, glorification—all these belong to us because the Holy Spirit has united us with Jesus. Union with Jesus is a tremendous theological concept. But it's the work of the Holy Spirit indwelling us to authenticate and validate faith by making the theological realities of salvation something tangible, something observable to the believer and to those around the believer.

In first century commerce, a seal was made by placing melted wax on a purchased possession and then cutting an impression into the wax with a signet ring. The seal bore the identity of the

---

14. John Calvin, *Institutes of the Christian Religion*, John T. McNeil, ed., Ford Lewis Battles, trans. (Philadelphia: Westminster, 1960), III.i.1.

owner. Here's the picture. The image in the wax was something tangible. The Holy Spirit seals us or marks us as those belonging to God by stamping us, if you will, with the image of Jesus who purchased us. This is so awesome! The Holy Spirit sealing us and sanctifying us is the expression of His infinite delight and passion for the world to see Jesus. He is at work in expressing Jesus and making Jesus visible and tangible in the unique personality of every believer. Look at this:

> *Christ is the visible image of the invisible God.*
> —Col. 1:15 NLT

The Holy Spirit wants each and every redeemed rebel to be the medium by which He reveals Jesus, who is "the visible image of the invisible God." The truly Spirit-filled, Spirit-led life doesn't bear the initials H.S.—Holy Spirit. It bears the initials J.C.—Jesus Christ.

A lot of people are talking about spirituality, or being "spiritual." At the heart of false spirituality is the agenda of getting God to change, to conform Him to our image. True spirituality—Christianity—is about God the Holy Spirit making us more like God and conforming us to Jesus.

The Holy Spirit takes the reality of our union with Jesus and makes that union tangible. He leaves the stamp of His character upon our hearts and lives.

Here are a couple of practical points of application.

1. If being sealed with the Holy Spirit is proof of our redemption and if that work involves the Holy Spirit making the character of Jesus tangible to the world around us, what evidence is there in our lives that we have been sealed? That is a big part of assurance.
2. You could not affix the seal to hardened wax. It was only on soft wax that the impression could be made. The Holy

Spirit is relentlessly seeking to melt hard hearts so He can impress upon that heart the character of Jesus, which is God's mark of ownership. That is proof of redemption. God's mark of ownership is the expression of Jesus Christ in our lives.

The proof that we are the purchased possession of God is not a church logo sticker on a car window or bumper. The proof that we are the purchased possession of God is not a shirt that says "Not of the World" or a "HE>I" tattoo. It is the tangible expression of Jesus being more clearly stamped on our lives by the Holy Spirit.

Finally, the Holy Spirit living in us seals us—secures our ultimate and eternal salvation.

> *The Spirit is God's guarantee that he will give us the inheritance he promised and that he has purchased us to be his own people.*
>
> —Eph. 1:14 NLT

I like the language of the King James Version:

> *Ye were sealed with that holy Spirit of promise, which is the earnest of our inheritance.*
>
> —Eph. 1:13–14 KJV

Earnest = a pledge, such as part of the purchase money or property given in advance as security for the rest. We call it earnest money, the money you are willing to put down to prove you're committed to completing a transaction.

The entirety of our redemption has been paid for in full by Jesus (redemption through His blood). But there is a facet of our redemption that has yet to be realized—the laying aside of our mortal bodies.

*For we know that if the tent that is our earthly home
is destroyed, we have a building from God, a house
not made with hands, eternal in the heavens. For in
this tent we groan, longing to put on our heavenly
dwelling. For while we are still in this tent, we groan,
being burdened--not that we would be unclothed,
but that we would be further clothed, so that what is
mortal may be swallowed up by life.*

2 Cor. 5:1-2, 4

God wants you to know that He means to carry out the transaction of your redemption to its ultimate end. The property given
in advance as our security that He will complete the transaction
of redemption is the Holy Spirit, "who is the guarantee of our
inheritance until we acquire possession of it, to the praise of his
glory" (Eph. 1:13-14).

In fact, the Bible teaches that the Holy Spirit living in us is
God's guarantee of heaven. To guarantee that our faith in Jesus
really saves, that we're really going to get to heaven, God says He'll
come to live in us until we go to live forever with Him. Because
of that guarantee, Paul says, "So we are always of good courage"
(2 Cor. 5:6).

Why is it so crucial for us to know that a facet of our new and
true identity is that we are sealed? Because we don't always feel like
we're real Christians; we don't always feel like we're actually going
to make it to heaven. But the seal of the Spirit is there even when
we don't feel like it. Here's the picture. A couple of winters ago, a
big chunk of America was frozen, literally. Tons of lakes had ice on
them 1-2 feet thick. Some people walked out onto that thick ice,
but they acted like it was only 2 inches thick. They were paralyzed
by insecurity and fear, afraid to take another step because they felt
like they would fall through any moment. But 2 feet of ice is going

to hold you up even if you feel like it can't. So lace up your skates, get on the ice, and get in the game. You're secure!

God who can't lie tells us that the moment we believe with our heart on the Lord Jesus, He gives us the Holy Spirit. And the Holy Spirit seals us. He validates our faith and authenticates that we are the purchased possession of God. He guarantees that we will spend forever with Him in a new heaven and a new earth, all because of what God did in sending Jesus to save us. Every man and woman who has believed with their heart on the Lord Jesus can say, "I am sealed."

> Faith is not primarily a function of how you feel. Faith is living out what God has said to be true about you despite how you feel.

Faith moves us to yield ourselves to the sealing work of the Holy Spirit, yielding to Him even the hardest part of our hearts to be softened so He might stamp on us more fully and more clearly than ever before the image of Jesus.

chapter eight

understanding more about my standing in jesus

Ephesians 1:15–23

The Bible tells us *why* our world is broken and why *we* are broken. Everything broken in the world is rooted in people's choice to find their deepest sense of meaning and identity from something other than God, from created things rather than the Creator. That choice has left every human broken on every level.

Our sin and idolatry have left us broken in the vertical axis of our lives and has separated us from God here and now and for eternity. Our sin and idolatry have also left us broken on the horizontal axis of or lives. Our desperate search for identity and meaning in what we do, what we possess, and what we can control has resulted in collateral damage in every sphere of existence. It has left us broken spiritually, psychologically, socially, environmentally, and geopolitically.

The Bible not only tells *why* we are broken, but it also tells us *how* we can be rescued and made whole. The gospel is literally the announcement of news, the record of who Jesus is and what Jesus has done to save us. By way of His virgin birth, sinless life, and bodily resurrection, Jesus has made a way for us to be saved from the eternal and temporal consequences of our sin and idolatry. Jesus saves us to a new destiny and saves us to be forever in the presence of God. Jesus saves us to a new and true identity.

The Holy Spirit inspired Paul to write this amazing letter to Christians living in the city of Ephesus in the middle of the first century to connect the gospel to everyday life between the already and the not yet. He wrote it to tell us how our true identity is rooted in all God has done for us in, through, with, and by Jesus.

Here are the amazing truths that are in just the first 13 verses of Ephesians 1:

> I am in Christ.
> I am a saint (set apart to God and for God).
> I am blessed (the object of God's active love).
> I am chosen.
> I am holy, without blame.
> I am loved.
> I am adopted.
> I am accepted.
> I am redeemed.
> I am forgiven.
> I am safe in the plan of God.
> I am sealed by the Holy Spirit.

Paul isn't close to being finished with unpacking our new and true identity. But in Ephesians 1:15–23, Paul slams on the brakes. He can't go on. He is compelled to tell the believers in Ephesus how he prays for them. He prays that they will understand their standing in Jesus, understand the riches of their new relationship with God, and understand their new identity in Jesus.

> *For this reason, because I have heard of your faith in the Lord Jesus and your love toward all the saints, I do not cease to give thanks for you, remembering you in my prayers, that the God of our Lord Jesus Christ, the Father of glory, may give you a Spirit of wisdom and of revelation in the knowledge of him.*
>
> —Eph. 1:15–17

This isn't the only time we find Paul praying while he was in prison (see Eph. 1:15–23, 3:14–21, Phil. 1:9–11, Col. 1:9–12). The Holy Spirit was very intentional to record the fact that Paul prayed a lot for others while he was in prison. But He also wants us to know what Paul prayed for when he prayed for others. His prayer life is very informative. As we look at his prison prayers recorded for us in this specific passage, we see that he didn't ask God to change the Ephesians' physical circumstances or remove their adversity or persecution. Instead, he asked God to supply everything they needed in their relationship with God in every circumstance. His prayers had to do with spiritual perception and understanding the will and ways of God in the midst of circumstances. He didn't pray for the transformation of circumstances; he prayed for the transformation of character.

This is so incredibly relevant to us in the 21st century. Here were men and women who had trusted Jesus to save them. And as a result, they had come into a living relationship with God; they had come to know God personally. And they were continuing to trust Jesus and walk with Jesus. Time had proved their faith in Jesus to be real. Their Christianity wasn't just a passing emotion. News had come to Paul in a Roman prison that they really trusted Jesus. Jesus Christ was at the center of everything in their lives. Everything started with Jesus and ended with Jesus. Everything in their lives ran through Jesus. Jesus was the object of their trust and hope. They trusted Jesus utterly, entirely, and absolutely. Everything they had in relation to God was theirs *in* Jesus and *with* Jesus.

Paul had heard of their faith in the Lord Jesus and their love toward all the saints. They had walked with Jesus and served Jesus by loving others for Jesus and loving others to Jesus. Real faith in Jesus is transformational. Faith in who Jesus is and all Jesus has done to save you frees you to love others. Real love is the outcome of real faith.

Paul was constantly thanking God for the way the Ephesians had trusted Jesus to save them and had continued to trust in Jesus. He was thankful for the way their faith had resulted in their love for each other. But Paul desired them to know God more. How important was that to Paul? He said, "I do not cease to give thanks for you, remembering you in my prayers" (Eph. 1:16). It was so important to Paul that he constantly prayed for them that they might know their God and Savior more.

There's more of Jesus for us to know and experience than what we've experienced thus far. Paul's desire should be our desire. We should be desiring to know God more. That was Paul's personal desire. He considered everything as rubbish that he might know Jesus (Phil. 3:8). We should desire to know Him more. That is at the very core of why the local church exists. It's the body of Christ building itself up in love. "Grow in the grace and knowledge of our Lord and Savior Jesus Christ" (2 Pet. 3:18). Warren Wiersbe said, "To know God personally is salvation (John 17:3). To know Him increasingly is sanctification (Phil. 3:10). To know Him perfectly is glorification (1 Cor. 13:9–12)."[15]

---

15. Warren W. Wiersbe, *The Bible Exposition Commentary, Volume 2* (Wheaton, IL: Victor Books, 1996), 15.

Paul knows that the reality of the gospel can never be connected to everyday life by way of human deduction.

> *No eye has seen, no ear has heard, and no mind has imagined what God has prepared for those who love him.*
> —1 Cor. 2:9 NLT

In other words, we can't grasp our new destiny and our new identity by way of mere human intellect or intuition. Though we exercise our mind and our will in the matter of salvation, salvation is beyond us. Our salvation is by the Spirit, through the Son, and to the Father. The same holds true when it comes to the understanding and application of our salvation.

> *But it was to us that God revealed these things by his Spirit. For his Spirit searches out everything and shows us God's deep secrets.*
> —1 Cor. 2:10 NLT

The only why we are going to understand our standing in Jesus is by the Holy Spirit.

> *For who knows a person's thoughts except the spirit of that person, which is in him? So also no one comprehends the thoughts of God except the Spirit of God. Now we have received not the spirit of the world, but the Spirit who is from God, that we might understand the things freely given us by God.*
> —1 Cor. 2:11–12

Paul constantly prayed that God would give the believers at Ephesus spiritual wisdom and insight so they could grow in their knowledge of God. He told them about their standing in Jesus, but he was also constantly praying for them to understand their standing in Jesus, "having the eyes of your hearts enlightened" (Eph. 1:18). I love the way the New Living Translation states it: "I pray that your hearts will be flooded with light so that you can understand."

A fallen culture thinks of the heart as the emotional part of a person, but in the Bible, the heart is the center of who a person is. From it and by it he thinks (Rom. 1:21) and chooses and behaves and speaks (Matt. 12, Luke 6). The inability to see and understand spiritual things is not a matter of intelligence; it's a problem of the heart. The eyes of the heart must be opened by the Spirit of God.

A lot of people think that getting "revelation" is something that happens in the midst of some super-emotional, super-ecstatic spiritual experience. It can be. But most often it isn't. Remember, Paul wrote this letter from prison (Eph. 3:1, 4:1, 6:20).

This amazing letter came from a hard time. Fallen culture doesn't view hard times as the source of hope. Prison is not synonymous with hope. When you're feeling hopeless, you don't stop and say, "If I could just get into prison, I think I might get a totally renewed sense of hope." Paul was in chains, and those chains did not define God or interrupt Paul's hope. Paul's circumstances didn't change what he believed about God.

It was while Paul was in chains that he penned these words in Ephesians. Some believe it was Tychicus who wrote as Paul dictated. Others think that more likely than not, Paul dictated that one run-on sentence that is filled with some of the weightiest, most important theological concepts while he was chained to a Roman soldier. He was so secure in who God is and the eternal work of Jesus Christ that he was okay sitting in those chains. And it was in those chains that Paul spoke well of God.

This is huge! Paul could write these words in prison because he had personally experienced the reality of the very things he was praying for the Ephesians. Prisms refract light. Light passes through the prism and enables us to see the properties of that light, the various colors contained in it. The Holy Spirit turned a prison into the prism through which God flooded Paul's heart with light and enabled him to understand more and more who God is. Paul came to know that being in prison had not changed and never could change who God is.

Sometimes the Holy Spirit uses a season of darkness to flood our hearts with the light of who Jesus is. Do you know that it was a solar eclipse that enabled astronomers to photograph the light of the sun being bent by gravity, confirming Einstein's theory of relativity? The moon obscured the great majority of the sun's light, which enabled them to see the brilliant light of the sun as it had never before been seen. Scientists understood more about light than ever before because of that darkness. Sometimes, perhaps even most times, the Holy Spirit uses the prism of a prison—the eclipse of adversity, trial, or heartbreak—to flood our hearts with a greater and deeper personal understanding of Jesus.

The man in prison was writing about hope. It was not the kind of hope that a man in jail might have about an early release. Don't confuse the biblical concept of hope with culture's concept of hope. When culture talks of hope, it means to hope *for something*, such as "I hope there's money in this birthday card." The biblical concept of hope has to do with assurance for the future. Hope in Scripture is the absolute certainty of eternal life.

When we were without Jesus, outside of Jesus, we were without hope in this world (Eph. 2:12), but in Jesus Christ, we have a "living hope" (1 Pet. 1:3). That living hope is absolutely certain because it is anchored in Jesus's victory over sin and death.

> *Blessed be the God and Father of our Lord Jesus Christ!*
> *According to his great mercy, he has caused us to be*
> *born again to a living hope through the resurrection*

of Jesus Christ from the dead, to an inheritance that is imperishable, undefiled, and unfading, kept in heaven for you, who by God's power are being guarded through faith for a salvation ready to be revealed in the last time. Though you have not seen him, you love him. Though you do not now see him, you believe in him and rejoice with joy that is inexpressible and filled with glory, obtaining the outcome of your faith, the salvation of your souls.

—1 Pet. 1:3–5, 8–9

Paul the prisoner had hope, not the kind of hope a man in jail might have about an early release. Paul was filled with a living hope, a hope that shaped the way he lived and the way he understood present adversity. That hope sustained him even in shackles. He wanted the Ephesians to know "the riches of his glorious inheritance in the saints" (Eph. 1:18).

Paul wants us to know that every redeemed rebel is God's glorious inheritance. How did Paul manage prison? He knew that his chains didn't change or disprove the fact that he was God's glorious inheritance. He took comfort and found joy in the fact that he personally was the very thing Jesus died to obtain. What does God get for sending His Son to die on a cross? Us!

Paul went on to say, "and what is the immeasurable greatness of his power toward us who believe" (Eph. 1:19). Again, this is Paul from prison. A man at the mercy of the might and power of Caesar is exhausting the Greek language to explain to the Ephesians the might and power of God to us and for us, right here and right now.

The word translated *immeasurable* is *huperballon* in Greek, or literally "a throwing beyond." It was used to describe something that was beyond measure, beyond comprehension, and more than enough. Paul wrings out the Greek vocabulary to get his point across to the believer concerning the power of God at work in the life of every believer. Let's look at some of those Greek words.

dunamis – power, as in dynamo and dynamite
energeia – working, as in energy
kratos – mighty
ischus – power

Kenneth Wuest translated verse 19 like this: "And what is the superabounding greatness of His inherent power to us who are believing ones as measured by the operative energy of the manifested strength of His might."[16] Warren Wiersbe translated it this way: "What is the surpassing greatness of His power toward us who believe, according to the operation of the might of His strength."[17]

This is divine dynamic, eternal energy that is available to us so we can live in our new and true identity and live out our new and true identity. We have the power to evangelize, the power to endure hardship, the power to overcome sin, the power to overcome temptation, the power to do God's will, the power to serve, and the power to speak.

Now let's look at the benchmark, the reference point, of His power.

According to the working of his great might that he worked in Christ when he raised him from the dead and seated him at his right hand in the heavenly places.
—Eph. 1:19–20

16. Kenneth S. Wuest, *Wuest's Word Studies from the Greek New Testament, Volume 1* (Grand Rapids, MI: Wm B. Eerdmans, 1973), 54–55.
17. Warren Wiersbe, *The Bible Exposition Commentary, Volume 2* (Wheaton, IL: Victor Books, 1996), 16.

The power God makes available to the believer is the same power that raised Christ from the dead (the power of the resurrection) and seated Him at God's right hand in heaven (the power of the ascension). The same power that took Jesus from the grave to glory is working in us right now. And one day this same power is going to do for us what it did for Jesus.

Don't miss this. Paul isn't praying that God gives us this power. He is praying that we have a divine awareness of the power that is a part of who we are in Jesus and part of our standing in Jesus.

His divine power has granted to us all things that pertain to life and godliness, through the knowledge of him who called us to his own glory and excellence, by which he has granted to us his precious and very great promises, so that through them you may become partakers of the divine nature, having escaped from the corruption that is in the world because of sinful desire.

—2 Pet. 1:3–4

Peter is saying that God, the Creator of the universe, the one who measures the universe with the span of His hand, has granted unto us "all things that pertain to life and godliness" according to His power.

Paul not only wants us to understand the greatness of the power of God that is exercised toward us and that is available to us, but He also wants us to understand the greatness of Jesus.

Far above all rule and authority and power and dominion, and above every name that is named, not only in this age but also in the one to come.

—Eph. 1:21

The more we understand who Jesus is, the more we understand who we are in Him. Jesus is:

Far above all rule
Far above all authority
Far above all power
Far above all dominion
Far above every name that is named

Do we live as though that's who Jesus is? Think about people's reaction to the last presidential election. Then think of Paul, Peter, and other Christians living under the reign of Nero, the Roman emperor.

And he put all things under his feet and gave him as head over all things to the church, which is his body, the fullness of him who fills all in all.

—Eph. 1:22–23

By telling me who Jesus is—"head over all things to the church"—Paul is also telling me who I am. I'm a member of His body on earth, subject to His will and His desires. When a member of the human body isn't subject to the directions and impulses of the brain, they have spastic movement. It is inefficient and uncoordinated, and it's hard to watch. That's how the church works and how the church is seen when the members of the body of Christ fail to understand who Jesus is and who they are. I'm in great need to understand more about my standing in Jesus.

Christians, the church is "his body, the fullness of him who fills all in all" (Eph. 1:23). What a statement!

When Solomon was dedicating the Temple, he said, "But will God indeed dwell on the earth? Behold, heaven and the highest heaven cannot contain you" (1 Kings 8:27).

Paul wrote, "For in Him dwells all the fullness of the Godhead bodily; and you are complete in Him, who is the head of all principality and power" (Col. 2:9–10 NKJV) and "that you may be filled with all the fullness of God" (Eph. 3:19). In His High Priestly Prayer the night before He died, Jesus said, "I in them and You in Me" (John 17:23).

We live in a day when a lot of people understand a few things about Christian subculture, about a particular church, how they think that church fits them, and how they think they fit in that church. That is not what we need to understand. We need the Holy Spirit to help us understand who Jesus is so we can understand who we are.

chapter nine

who i was – who i am – why he did it – how he did it

Ephesians 2:1–10

In Ephesians Chapter 2, keep in mind that it's easy for us to think of Ephesians as a book. We call it the book of Ephesians. We refer to it as the 50th book of the Bible. But it was written as a letter. It had no chapter divisions and no verse references. What we call the first 10 verses of Chapter 2 is actually another incredibly long sentence. Paul intentionally wants the first three verses of this second long sentence to stand in utter and absolute contrast to the first long sentence in Chapter 1. The first long sentence describes our new and true identity—who we are in Jesus. In the first three verses of the second long sentence of his letter, Paul juxtaposes our election and adoption, our redemption and forgiveness, and the life-giving, life-changing resurrection power of God with who we *were* without Jesus.

He takes us to a place where we understand that this thing the Bible calls *grace* is not merely a concept or a sentiment; it is something more *real* and more *amazing* than we could ever imagine. God has really done something. He has done something for us that we don't deserve and could never earn. That's what grace is. We can never understand how gracious grace is until we understand the sinfulness of sin.

> We can never understand how saved we are until we understand how lost we were.

If you go to buy a diamond, the jeweler first lays down a black background on top of the display case and then sets the diamond on it. It is against the contrast of the black backdrop that you can see the brilliance of the diamond. Paul wants us to see the amazing brilliance and beauty of this thing called grace so he sets our new identity in Jesus against the black backdrop of our old identity.

In this one long sentence that begins Ephesians 2, Paul explains how the gospel takes us from death to life, from the graveyard to glory.

Verses 1–3 – Who we were
Verses 4–6 – Who we are
Verse 7 – Why He did it
Verses 8–9 – How He did it
Verse 10 – Who we are

This is us on the black backdrop of who we were.

And you were dead in the trespasses and sins in which you once walked, following the course of this world, following the prince of the power of the air, the spirit

*that is now at work in the sons of disobedience—
among whom we all once lived in the passions of our
flesh, carrying out the desires of the body and the
mind, and were by nature children of wrath, like the
rest of mankind.*

—Eph. 2:1–3

Here's the broad stroke:

We were without life.
We were without freedom.
We were without hope.
We were dead.

As we move through these first three verses of Chapter 2, note the tense of the verbs. The first verb in this long sentence is *were* (past tense). That was our old state of being—dead is what we used to be.

Paul's diagnosis of man's condition is not in keeping with sociologists, psychologists, anthropologists, and humanists. They say we are a little misguided. They say we are a little culturally and socially deprived. They say humans' temporarily flawed condition can be changed, that given enough time and education and given the right environment, people will eventually become the best version of humans. God's diagnosis and prognosis aren't even close to that. *Dead* is a strong word.

Dead = without life. Jesus said that He came so we might have life. He said that to men and women who were biologically alive. They were existing but not living. Everyone intuits that. It's why everyone is in a desperate search for some identity that will provide them a sense of being alive that transcends having a heartbeat and a brain wave.

Men and women organizing their lives without God and against God are not simply sick and needing a little help; they are actually dead people needing life. Dead people can't get better. They need a resurrection. They need life breathed into them. And that is beyond their capacity. *Dead* = powerless. Romans 5:6 (NLT) says "when we were utterly helpless."

Sin kills. It separates us from God, who is our life. Romans 6:23 says, "For the wages of sin is death." Ezekiel 18:20 says, "The soul who sins shall die."

Ephesians 2:1 says, "dead in the trespasses and sins."

Trespasses = wrong steps taken, deliberate breaking of the law, willful disobedience. Let's say someone draws a line and says, "Don't step over this line." You look at the line, you look at them, and then you step over that line. That is willful disobedience. That is exactly what Adam and Eve did in Genesis 3. That is exactly what all of us have done.

Sin = missing the mark. It is failing to live up to the standard of God's holiness.

Trespasses speak of us as rebels. Sins speak of us as failures. We were all "dead in the trespasses and sins in which you once walked." Don't miss this. Before coming to Jesus, rebelling and failing were the sphere in which we existed. That was our address before believing with our hearts on the Lord Jesus. It was the bent of our existence.

God's diagnosis explains why the world is broken. Dead things cause things around them to rot. If you strap a dead body to a prisoner, the rot of the corpse will start eating the flesh of the prisoner. Trespasses and sin are the cause of the spiritual death of the individual, and the spiritual death of individuals rots our culture.

We were dead, without life, and we were also without freedom. It was how we "once walked, following the course of this world, following the prince of the power of the air, the spirit that is now at work in the sons of disobedience" (Eph. 2:2).

Walk is often the biblical way of describing a way of life.

And he did what was right in the eyes of the Lord, and walked in the ways of David his father; and he did not turn aside to the right hand or to the left.

—2 Chron. 34:2

Because they have forsaken me and worshiped Ashtoreth the goddess of the Sidonians, Chemosh the god of Moab, and Milcom the god of the Ammonites, and they have not walked in my ways.

—1 Kings 11:33

Life is a walk, an active process that moves along step by step. In our old state of being when our trespasses and sins separated us from God who alone is our life, we walked, following the course of this world.

Walked = wandered aimlessly; meandered. There's a big difference between walked and meandered. Walk implies purpose; meander implies moving without purpose. This morning I had to go to the post office to mail my tax returns. I walked straight from my car to the post office. I didn't stop to look in any store windows. By contrast, some people meander when they go to the mall. They go from storefront to storefront to see if anything catches their eye or pulls them into the store. Before meeting Jesus, we were meandering, shopping for replacement identities.

We walked, following the course of this world. The word *course* is the word used to refer to a weather vane. A weather vane can't determine the direction it moves. It's moved by the prevailing winds. That is who we used to be, controlled by the values and attitudes of this world.

We were "following the course of this world, following the prince of the power of the air, the spirit that is now at work in the sons of disobedience" (Eph. 2:2). Paul tells us that behind the visible world there is an invisible world. Behind the course of this world is the prince of the power of the air.

Air = spiritual realm. The Bible refers to this superhuman, super-powerful entity as Satan. In 2 Corinthians 4:4, Paul called him the "god of this world." Jesus referred to him as "the ruler of this world" (John 16:11). We're told in 1 John 5:19 (NLT) that "the whole world around us is under the control of the evil one."

This prince of the power of the air is called "the spirit that is now at work in the sons of disobedience" (Eph. 2:2). The world at large and even at times Christians don't want to believe that there is a satanic influence in people's lives. But we must not think that Satan's work is only limited to acts of violence or pathological behavior. He is also at work in the faithful husband and dad when he gets him to become a religious moralist. The god of this world is at work in the hearts of men who disobey the truth. "In those days there was no king in Israel. Everyone did what was right in his own eyes" (Judges 21:25).

Ephesians 2:3 goes on to say, "among whom we all once lived in the passions of our flesh."

The "passions of our flesh" is the sinful "I want" of our fallen nature. Before being in Jesus, we were slaves to those "I want" desires.

Verse 3 then adds, "carrying out the desires of the body and the mind." We disobeyed God with our bodies. That refers to our disobedient and sinful actions. We disobeyed God with our minds. This is a reference to our sinful choices. The Message states it like this: "all of us doing what we felt like doing, when we felt like doing it, all of us in the same boat."

Verse 3 adds, "and were by nature children of wrath, like the rest of mankind."

Children = a close relationship to one's parents (Greek *tekna*) Without Jesus, we had a close relationship with God's wrath. The New American Standard Bible translates "children" as "objects." Without Jesus we were the objects of God's wrath. "Whoever believes in the Son has eternal life; whoever does not obey the Son shall not see life, but the wrath of God remains on him" (John 3:36). "The wrath of God is coming upon the sons of disobedience" (Col. 3:6 NKJV).

That is who we were by nature. That is who we were naturally and innately. Here's the point. We did not become sinners because we sinned; we sinned because we are sinners.

> We were without life – dead in sin.
> We were without freedom – influenced by Satan and controlled by lust.
> We were without hope – under God's wrath.

That is the black backdrop of who we were. Then Paul uses one of the most powerful words in the Bible in one of the most powerful phrases of the Bible to introduce how God changed us from who we were to who we are in, through, with, and by Jesus.

At the beginning of verse 4, we see a very important word—*but*. That little word means that everything that follows stands in stark contrast to everything that came before it. We were without life (dead in sin). We were without freedom (influenced by Satan, controlled by lust). We were without hope (under God's wrath). And then we see the words "but God."

> *But God* is rich in mercy.
> *But God* loved us.
> *But God* saved us.
> *But God* seated us with Christ.

Where sin increased, grace abounded all the more, so that, as sin reigned in death, grace also might reign through righteousness leading to eternal life through Jesus Christ our Lord.

—Rom. 5:20–21

Read Ephesians 2:4–6 from The Message:

We all did it, all of us doing what we felt like doing, when we felt like doing it, all of us in the same boat. It's a wonder God didn't lose his temper and do away with the whole lot of us. Instead, immense in mercy and with an incredible love, he embraced us. He took our sin-dead lives and made us alive in Christ. He did all this on his own, with no help from us! Then he picked us up and set us down in highest heaven in company with Jesus, our Messiah.

God is rich in mercy. He is not a one-dimensional God who is only a God of wrath. The word *mercy* speaks of emotion aroused by someone in need and the attempt to relieve the person and remove their trouble. It is our condition that moves God to be merciful.

Who we were evoked God's mercy. God saw us lifeless and powerless, decaying in bondage, blindly stepping in holes, and hopeless in the face of the wrath we deserved. That evoked His rich mercy.

"But God, being rich in mercy, because of the great love with which he loved us" (Eph. 2:4). His rich mercy is rooted in His "great love" for us. God's love is great beyond measure. The Bible quantifies His love with unquantifiable terms: He loves us with "an everlasting love" (Jer. 31:3). His love is measured in the unquantifiable terms of the divine action He took to save us—what it cost Him to take that action.

God does not love in the realm of mere sentiment or emotion. God doesn't just *feel* loving; He actually *does* love. He acts. Out of His very essence (God is love), He does and He acts. And it cost Him everything to take that action. He did something by sending Jesus to rescue us. "In this is love, not that we have loved God but that he loved us and sent his Son to be the propitiation [wrath-appeasing sacrifice] for our sins" (1 John 4:10). God's love is not a feeling. God's love is a choice. God made a choice to send His Son to save us when we couldn't save ourselves.

> *Even when we were dead in our trespasses, made us alive together with Christ.*
>
> —Eph. 2:5

We were dead — He made us alive. *Alive* = raised, kept alive, preserved life, quickened, granted a new spiritual life

> *By grace you have been saved.*
>
> —Eph. 2:5

The tense of the verb here is significant. It speaks of a completed action with a continuing result. Justin Alfred, who has spent his life studying biblical languages, put it this way: "By grace you are converted; are being kept, and by grace will go home to be with the Lord."

> *And raised us up with him and seated us with him in the heavenly places in Christ Jesus.*
>
> —Eph. 2:6

We have been united with Jesus in His resurrected life. Throughout this letter we are tethered to the opening words of the first verse of Chapter 1—*in Christ*. We are forever united with Jesus, forever identified with Jesus. What happened to Jesus will happen to us.

We were dead and doomed, but now we are alive and exalted.

Our redemption is complete. Jesus said, "It is finished" (John 19:30). It is a done deal. But we are waiting to experience the redemption of our bodies, the moment we receive a new body that is fit for the heavenlies, will never grow old, will never get sick, will never get tired, and will never fail. But while we are waiting for that, we are right now seated with Jesus in the heavenly places.

Warren Wiersbe said, "Our physical position may be on earth, but our spiritual position is 'in heavenly places in Christ Jesus.'"[18] There is a very real and practical application of this! We should live on earth with our hearts in heaven.

> *If then you have been raised with Christ, seek the things that are above, where Christ is, seated at the right hand of God. Set your minds on things that are above, not on things that are on earth. For you have died, and your life is hidden with Christ in God. When Christ who is your life appears, then you also will appear with him in glory. Put to death therefore what is earthly in you: sexual immorality, impurity, passion, evil desire, and covetousness, which is idolatry. On account of these the wrath of God is coming. In these you too once walked, when you were living in them. But now you must put them all away.*
>
> —Col. 3:1-8

---

18. Warren Wiersbe, *The Wiersbe Bible Commentary New Testament*, Google Books, 593.

Why did He do it? "So that in the coming ages he might show the immeasurable riches of his grace in kindness toward us in Christ Jesus" (Eph. 2:7).

Who we are in Jesus is seen against the pitch black backdrop of who we were. That will forever "show the immeasurable riches of his grace in kindness toward us in Christ Jesus" (Eph. 2:7).

How did He do it? How did we go from who we were (without life, without freedom, without hope) to who we are (loved, saved, seated in heavenly places with Jesus)?

> *For by grace you have been saved through faith. And this is not your own doing; it is the gift of God, not a result of works, so that no one may boast.*
>
> —Eph. 2:8–9

Saved—this is such a massive concept! It includes justification, reconciliation, adoption, and so much more. By grace you have been saved. Mercy, love, and grace—that's our God.

Grace = God's riches at Christ's expense, getting what we do not deserve. We couldn't climb up to heaven, so God came down for us.

Salvation = 100% God

By grace we are saved through faith. Faith is not a work that earns us salvation. It is the channel through which salvation is received. Believing with your heart on the Lord Jesus connects you with the saving work that Jesus accomplished for you, something you could never earn and don't deserve.

> *Saving is all his idea, and all his work. All we do is trust him enough to let him do it. It's God's gift from start to finish! We don't play the major role. If we did, we'd probably go around bragging that we'd*

done the whole thing! No, we neither make nor save
ourselves. God does both the making and saving.

—Eph. 2:8–9 MSG

Who we are is because of what He did.

For we are his workmanship, created in Christ Jesus
for good works, which God prepared beforehand, that
we should walk in them.

—Eph. 2:10

We have been redeemed, raised, reconciled, and recreated for a new purpose—His workmanship. "If anyone is in Christ, he is a new creation" (2 Cor. 5:17). In Christ—once again—Jesus is the repository of all that is ours as believers. Everything that is ours in relationship to God is ours in Jesus and with Jesus.

Again, we can only truly understand this element of our new and true identity in light of who we were.

And you were dead in the trespasses and sins in which
you once walked, following the course of this world,
following the prince of the power of the air, the spirit that
is now at work in the sons of disobedience—among whom
we all once lived in the passions of our flesh, carrying out
the desires of the body and the mind, and were by nature
children of wrath, like the rest of mankind.

—Eph. 2:1–3

That is who I was. That is who you were. And that is who we still would be if we hadn't seen the words *but God*.

In verse 10, the word translated "workmanship" is *poiema*. Remember that word from which we get our word *poem*, the work of art?

In Jesus, I am God's handcrafted work of art.

My identity in Jesus tells me that conversion is not the end; it is the beginning.

Right now God is making something beautiful of my life so I can be part of His work in the world, resulting in His glory. I am going to become all He saved me to be in Christ. "He creates each of us by Christ Jesus to join him in the work he does, the good work he has gotten ready for us to do, work we had better be doing" (Eph. 2:10 MSG).

chapter ten

i am reconciled – i am a new person

Ephesians 2:11–18

Paul opened his letter to the Christians in Ephesus with one long sentence (Eph. 1:3–14). If Ephesians is the Mount Everest of the Bible, that single sentence is like the peak of Everest. In that single sentence we find out who we are as the Holy Spirit unpacks and explains all that is involved in the redeeming, reconciling, and restoring work of Jesus.

Predestination — Adoption — Redemption — Forgiveness — Sealing of the Holy Spirit — Imperishable Hope — Regeneration — Immeasurable Power

In Chapter 2, Paul opened with another long sentence. With the first three verses of this second long sentence, Paul juxtaposes our election and adoption, our redemption and forgiveness, and the life-giving, life-changing resurrection power of God with who we were without Jesus.

God wants us understand that this thing the Bible calls *grace* is not merely a concept or sentiment. It is something more *real* and more *amazing* than we could ever imagine. God really has done something! He is the one who has done *everything* to save us, and we didn't deserve any of it and could never earn it. That is what grace is. We can *never* understand how gracious grace is until we understand how sinful sin is. We can *never* understand how saved we are until we understand how lost we were. With this one long sentence, Paul explains how the gospel takes us from death to life, from the graveyard to glory.

We were without life — dead in sin.

We were without freedom — influenced by Satan, sinners by nature, and controlled by lust.

We were without hope — under God's wrath with no way of escape.

It's against that pitch-black backdrop that Paul uses one of the most powerful words in the Bible, and he uses it in one of the most powerful phrases of the Bible to introduce how God changed us from who we were to who we are in, through, with, and by Jesus. That little word *but* means that everything that follows it stands in stark contrast to everything that came before it. And the phrase is *but God* (Eph. 2:4).

> *But God* is rich in mercy.
> *But God* loved us.
> *But God* saved us.
> *But God* seated us with Christ.

Up to Ephesians 2:10 Paul has been unpacking and explaining the message of the gospel as it relates to all of lost humanity. But in Ephesians 2:11, Paul begins to explain specifically what the gospel means for anyone who is not Jewish. Remember, all the letters in the New Testament were written for a specific purpose to a specific group of people. Most of the men and women of Ephesus who had come to know Jesus weren't Jewish, but they understood through Paul's teaching ministry that the story of God's rescue mission was contained in and foretold by the Jewish Scriptures (the Old Testament).

From the beginning of the Book of Beginnings (Genesis), we have the introduction and unfolding of God's glorious plan to redeem and rescue us from the earth-shattering and eternal consequences of what has been called "cosmic treason," or overthrowing the rule of the very One who made us. Beginning in Genesis 12, we find that God's rescue plan was going to run through the descendants of a man named Abraham. His descendants would eventually come to be known as the nation of Israel. In an ethnic sense, that people group would be the "womb" through which the Savior of the world would come. That's why God told Abraham that "in your offspring shall all the nations of the earth be blessed" (Gen. 22:18). In fact, Jesus said that "salvation is from the Jews" (John 4:22).

This is really important for us if we are going to have context for what Paul is saying. The descendants of Abraham were uniquely the people of God. The Jews really are God's chosen people.

> For you are a holy people, who belong to the Lord your God. Of all the people on earth, the LORD your God has chosen you to be his own special treasure.
>
> —Deut. 7:6 NLT

They are uniquely the people of God, and among all the people groups in the world, they are incredibly privileged.

They are the people of Israel, chosen to be God's adopted children. God revealed his glory to them. He made covenants with them and gave them his law. He gave them the privilege of worshiping him and receiving his wonderful promises.

—Rom. 9:4 NLT

The covenant God made with Abraham was symbolized through circumcision. Later, the Law of Moses commanded that every male descendant of Abraham be circumcised on the eighth day after birth. The Jews looked at the world around them in terms of circumcision and uncircumcision. Remember the words of David the shepherd boy when he saw the giant Goliath taunting the Israelites? "For who is this uncircumcised Philistine, that he should defy the armies of the living God?" (1 Sam. 17:26).

Here's how David processed the world. There were those who uniquely belonged to and worshiped the true and living God. The physical mark of that special relationship was circumcision. And there were those who had no relationship with the true and living God. They had no mark of special relationship with the God of Abraham. They worshiped idols. This giant, Goliath, and the rest of the Philistine army had no physical mark of that special relationship with God, and they were daring to confront an army of men who were special to God.

God had already called Abraham, making a difference between Jews and Gentiles. He set them apart and marked their unique ethnic status through circumcision. He also set them apart by the laws He gave them at Mount Sinai. He told them how they were to worship Him, where they were to worship Him, and who would lead them in their worship. Through them God gave the world the inspired Scriptures of the Old Testament.

Don't miss this: they never did anything to earn that unique relationship with the living God. All of it had everything to do with grace, starting with the progenitor of the nation, Abraham. He was an idol worshiper in a pagan land. He wasn't seeking God, but God appeared to him for no other reason than to declare that His rescue plan was going to run through that man's descendants.

This is crucial. God made this difference between the descendants of Abraham and the rest of the world, not so the Jews could boast about being superior to non-Jewish people but so they would be a blessing and a help to the Gentiles. On more than one occasion in the Old Testament, God said that the nation of Israel was to be a light to the nations. God set them apart that He might use them to be a light to the Gentiles. God wanted to reveal His nature and goodness to the Gentile world through the Jews.

But here in Ephesians 2, we're told that this unique and privileged people went horribly wrong. In verses 14 and verse 16, we find the word *hostility*. The word Paul uses in both verses means *hate*. Their uniqueness and the privileges that were supposed to be a blessing to the rest of the world became the source of their hostility. The Jews came to despise (hate) the Gentiles because they weren't circumcised and didn't have the Law. The Gentiles did what comes naturally to fallen people when they are hated. They came to despise (hate) the Jews for hating them.

How did that happen? We talked about this very thing when we were laying the groundwork for our study of this book. We learned that when we refuse to find our deepest sense of meaning in God, we look for a replacement identity. Then, to protect and reinforce that false identity, we attach ourselves to others who have the same replacement identity. We use the term *tribe* to define those groups. Then we make an idol of our tribe and demonize other tribes.

Every Jew and the nation of Israel as a whole were to find their deepest sense of meaning in the true and living God who had made them unique among all the nations, made covenants with them, gave them His Law, gave them the privilege of worshiping Him, and gave them wonderful promises. They made an idol out of their unique and privileged ethnic status. They found their identity in being God's chosen people instead of finding their identity in the God who chose them.

Look at this incredibly twisted shift. Circumcision, the thing that was intended to represent their unique relationship with God, took the place of God. They defined themselves as those who were circumcised and thought of themselves as the circumcision. Nothing else mattered. Without circumcision, a person was nothing. The very gifts God had given them took the place of God in their lives. "We are circumcised," they boasted. "We have God's Law. We have the temple."

Here's how deceiving our replacement identities can be. Those of the circumcision had failed miserably as those who were to belong to God, to be faithful to the true and living God. On a national level, they acted like serial adulterers. For centuries, the circumcision (Jews) assumed the posture of being spiritually and morally superior to the non-Jewish world. The blessings of God became the lofty perch from which they looked down with disgust on the uncircumcision (Gentiles). William Barclay gives us this historical portrait of the circumcision:

> The Jew had an immense contempt for the Gentile. The Gentiles, said the Jews, were created by God to be fuel for the fires of hell. God, they said, loves only Israel of all the nations that he had made. . . . It was not even lawful to render help to a Gentile mother in her hour of sorest need, for that would simply be

to bring another Gentile into the world. Until Christ came, the Gentiles were an object of contempt to the Jews. The barrier between them was absolute. If a Jewish boy married a Gentile girl, or if a Jewish girl married a Gentile boy, the funeral of that Jewish boy or girl was carried out. Such contact with a Gentile was the equivalent of death.[19]

The division between Jew and Gentile seemed absolute. The very idea of reconciliation seemed absurd. It seemed beyond possibility that those who so utterly and completely despised each other could even in the smallest way be reconciled, let alone be found worshiping and adoring the same God and Savior.

Paul frames the gospel in terms of circumcision and uncircumcision so we see the transformational power of the gospel and see how the power of the gospel destroys historic hostilities and tears down the walls of hatred and bigotry.

But now in Christ Jesus you who once were far off have been brought near by the blood of Christ.

—Eph. 2:13

Paul doesn't say the Jews and Gentiles were finally brought near because they adopted a love-thy-neighbor ethic. They weren't brought near because they sat down at the negotiating table and found some tiny piece of common ground. No, Paul says they were brought near by the blood of Jesus. How does

---

19. William Barclay, *The Letters to the Galatians and Ephesians* (Louisville, KY: Westminster John Knox Press, 2002), 123.

the shed blood of Jesus bring together two groups divided by centuries of hostility? Here's how: the gospel gathers everyone into one group. Martyn Lloyd-Jones said, "We are all condemned felons before a holy God. He brings us down together to the dust."[20]

The gospel brings me face to face with Jesus. Jesus on the cross tells me the truth about myself. I'm that bad. My sins did that to the sinless Son of God.

Vertical reconciliation precedes and produces horizontal-human reconciliation.

The gospel is first and foremost about fixing what is broken between God and mankind. David, the king of Israel, understood this. After committing adultery and murder, he confessed, "For I know my transgressions, and my sin is ever before me. Against you, you only, have I sinned and done what is evil in your sight" (Ps. 51:3–4).

Every destructive word, attitude, and action in human history is the outcome of humans' refusal to be governed by God. Timothy Keller put it like this:

> Sin is like treason. If you try to overthrow your own country you may harm or kill individuals in the process, but you will be tried for treason because you have betrayed the entire country that nurtured you. So every sin is cosmic treason—it is overthrowing the rule of the one to whom you owe everything.[21]

---

20. D. Martyn Lloyd-Jones, *God's Way of Reconciliation: An Exposition of Ephesians 2* (Grand Rapids, MI: Baker Books, 1972), 162.
21. Timothy Keller and Kathy Keller, *The Songs of Jesus: A Year of Daily Devotions in the Psalms*, Google Books, 108.

Ephesians 2:17 says, "And he came and preached peace to you who were far off and peace to those who were near." The Gentiles were far from God. They didn't have God's law. They didn't have the Old Testament Scriptures. They had no moral restraint. They were really a mess. The Jews were near. The Jews had the Law of God, the Word of God, the tabernacle, and later the temple. This verse says both of them needed to hear the gospel of peace, both of them needed to be reconciled to God, and both were estranged from God and needed to be saved. That is one of the most radical things the gospel tells us.

Jesus on the cross made circumcision and uncircumcision irrelevant. There is only one group of humanity: sinners. Every tribe is made up of sinners who need the same grace. Every tribe is made up of sinners who need the same mercy. Every tribe is made up of sinners who need the same love. I'm no longer defined by my race, my age, my gender, my nationality, or any other thing that culture might use to categorize me. I see that I'm a sinner who needs a Savior.

For through him we both have access in one Spirit to the Father. So then you [Gentiles] are no longer strangers and aliens [outside of the covenant and promises of God], but you are fellow citizens with the saints and members of the household of God.
—Eph. 2:18–19

When a man or woman believes with their heart on the Lord Jesus, something radical happens. People who were once divided by deep-seated hatred and bigotry are brought near because the blood of Jesus has brought them both near to God. They are near to each other because they are both in the arms of God. The gospel creates a new kind of humanity, a new people group held together by the fact that they are *all* in Christ.

*Instead of continuing with two groups of people
separated by centuries of animosity and suspicion,
he created a new kind of human being, a fresh start
for everybody. Christ brought us together through his
death on the cross. The Cross got us to embrace, and
that was the end of the hostility.*

—Eph. 2:15–18 MSG

When someone becomes a Christian, their genetic information isn't changed. They still have the same biological, racial, and ethnic components. They aren't lifted out of one socioeconomic context or one national or cultural context and placed into one big homogenous box with other Christians.

Even though ethnic and cultural differences can still be distinguishable, they no longer define us. The blood of Jesus changes all of that. Because you are a new person in Jesus, you no longer identify yourself primarily on the basis of being a Jew or Gentile, black or white, Asian or Hispanic, Native American or any other ethnic group you can name. None of those things define the authentic Christian. They have a new identity: I am a new person in Jesus.

Jesus really does change everything. Our new relationship with Jesus brings about a deep and personal transformation that begins to affect change in culture—change in relationships that have been historically fractured and seemingly beyond repair.

Here's how. Keller points out how studies show that shared race and culture is a profound thing that affects almost every area of our life. In Jesus we experience in a very real and life-changing way a union with other Christians that is closer than genetics or genealogy, race or culture.

When you become a Christian, you're not just a little different. In one of his letters, Paul says that if you are in Jesus, you are a whole new creation. Paul says that if you are in Jesus, you are a new kind of human.

Because of our union with Jesus, we are called to process race, culture, and gender in a whole new way. Conventional wisdom says that one of the main reasons there is so much social unrest, division, and bigotry is because we need to develop a greater sensitivity to ethnic and cultural distinctions. Yet the more cultural distinctions are emphasized, the less we seem to get along. Galatians 3:28 says, "There is neither Jew nor Greek, there is neither slave nor free, there is no male and female, for you are all one in Christ Jesus." Paul isn't abolishing ethnicity, gender, or social status. He is saying that none of those things define the Christian. Paul says it again in his letter to the Colossians.

> *Here there is not Greek and Jew, circumcised and uncircumcised, barbarian, Scythian, slave, free; but Christ is all, and in all. Put on then, as God's chosen ones, holy and beloved, compassionate hearts, kindness, humility, meekness, and patience, bearing with one another and, if one has a complaint against another, forgiving each other; as the Lord has forgiven you, so you also must forgive. And above all these put on love, which binds everything together in perfect harmony.*
>
> —Col. 3:11–14

The gospel really does connect with everyday life. Because of Jesus we are freed from the replacement identities and the tribal mentalities they've produced throughout history that breed division, hatred, and bigotry. In Christ we can actually appreciate diversity and at the same time live in deep unity because we understand that *how* we do life is nothing compared to *who* Jesus is and *what* He has done to reconcile us—first to God and then to one another. The gospel reorders the way a man or woman relates to every individual and every tribe.

> The gospel humbles us out of our replacement identities and our tribal arrogance.

God didn't send Jesus to die on the cross for this race or that race. Jesus was nailed to a cross for the human race.

> *After this I looked, and behold, a great multitude which no one could number, from every nation, from all tribes and peoples and languages, standing before the throne and before the Lamb, clothed with white robes, with palm branches in their hands, and crying out with a loud voice, "Salvation belongs to our God who sits on the throne, and to the Lamb!"*
>
> —Rev. 7:9–10

Hebrews 2:11 says that Jesus is not ashamed to call us brothers. Jesus, the perfect version of humanity, didn't treat us as inferior. He went to the cross, and he was not ashamed to call us brothers and sisters. That should reshape the way we think of what our church should look like and who should be in our church. That should reshape the way we look at our mission in this world. Do we pray for, love on, and reach out to those we least identify with?

chapter eleven

i am a citizen – i am a child of god

Ephesians 2:19–22

So far we have learned that the gospel is so powerful and so transformational that it is able to reconcile people who have been divided for centuries by hate and prejudice. That horizontal reconciliation is rooted in and preceded by vertical reconciliation.

> *But now in Christ Jesus you who once were far off have been brought near by the blood of Christ. For he himself is our peace.*
>
> —Eph. 2:13–14

I can never overstate how essential the Word of God is to our lives and our relationships. Without it we could never know who we are in Jesus. God hasn't left it up to us to figure out our dream about what a Christian is or isn't. He wants us to be transformed by the renewing of our minds. The Word of God changes the way we live because it tells us who God is, who we are, and the truth about our fallen culture. If we understand who we are in Christ, we will have some understanding of what to do in our circumstances and problems.

There are a lot of professing Christians who consistently struggle with anxieties, fears, and hostilities that prevent them from acting as God intended human beings to act. A lot of them go to church but only hear about certain sections of the Bible that are dished out like servings of chicken soup for the soul. They think of God as their life coach and that the Bible is a book of advice. The Bible is not a book about humans. It is a book about God. It is the revelation of God to mankind. People are anxious and fearful because they have no clear understanding of God. In the Bible, people are seen relative to God. Gospel living is rooted in gospel truth.

Paul has been telling who Jesus is and what Jesus has done so we can understand who we are in Him. Christians are new kinds of humans because they are in Jesus. That new kind of humanity is not theory; it is real and tangible. Paul is defining what this new kind of human looks like.

Ephesians 2:19 begins with the words "so then," or consequently, as a consequence of being in Jesus. Our new and true identity in Jesus is deep and profound. It is layered and beautifully complex, not complicated but intricate in, with, through, and by Jesus.

> I am a saint – set apart to God and for God.
> I am blessed – the object of God's active love.
> I am chosen.
> I am holy.
> I am without blame.
> I am loved.

I am adopted.

I am accepted.

I am redeemed.

I am forgiven.

I am safe in the plan of God.

I am sealed by the Holy Spirit.

I am God's inheritance.

I am God's workmanship.

I am reconciled.

I am part of a new kind of humanity.

The opening words of Ephesians 2:19 tell us that *all* of those truths are leading to something.

> *So then you are no longer strangers and aliens, but you are fellow citizens with the saints and members of the household of God, built on the foundation of the apostles and prophets, Christ Jesus himself being the cornerstone, in whom the whole structure, being joined together, grows into a holy temple in the Lord.*
>
> —Eph. 2:19–21

Because our identity in Jesus is so nuanced, so layered, and so wonderfully complex, the Bible has to use more than one metaphor to describe it. The Bible tells us that Jesus is the Good Shepherd. That metaphor is loaded with practical truth and life applications. It not only explains the heart of Jesus and the work of Jesus, but it explains who I am. I'm like a sheep. The greatest need of a sheep is to have a shepherd. As Shepherd, Jesus leads; as one of His sheep, I follow. As Shepherd, Jesus feeds; as one of His sheep, I look to Him to nourish my soul. Because Jesus is Shepherd, the Bible speaks about us as sheep, and collectively we are His flock.

At the close of Ephesians 2, Paul describes our new and true identity in Jesus in terms of three distinct figures. They follow each other, each building on the previous one. They are packed with truth about who we are in Jesus.

> Verse 19 – "Fellow citizens with the saints." This is the image of a *kingdom*.
> Verse 19 – "Members of the household of God." This is the image of a *family*.
> Verse 21 – "In whom the whole structure, being joined together, grows into a holy temple in the Lord." This is the image of a *building*.

Paul uses these images to speak of reality. There is a literal reality in the word pictures Paul is painting. They define the reality of who we are. The truth of who we are in Jesus transforms the way we think and live on this side of eternity.

The Image of a Kingdom

A stranger is characterized as not knowing much about where they are. In 1990 my family moved from our home that was 15 minutes from the beach in Southern California to the town of Grass Valley in the foothills of the Sierra Nevada Mountains in Northern California. It didn't take us long to discover that we were strangers and aliens. We had no idea where anything was. Where do we shop, eat out, and hang out? We had no idea about how to get around on the roads. There wasn't anything familiar to us about life in the foothills with its flannel shirts, buck knives, cowboy boots, and pickup trucks.

Strangers are ignorant. Before we met Jesus, we were strangers. We didn't know the first thing about God. We didn't know the first thing about His capacity to meet us in our failures, phobias, and hostilities. Now that we have come to Christ, we are no longer strangers to God's peace, God's power, and God's provision.

To be an alien is far more than feeling like you don't belong. An alien is someone with no ultimate rights. They don't have a birth certificate that makes them a citizen of a country. That's an accurate picture of a lot of people who grew up (or are growing up) in a Christian family and go to church with some regularity. They're familiar with the language of Christianity, but they've never become a Christian. They're foreigners living on a passport. They haven't experienced the full rights and privileges of being a full-born citizen in the Kingdom of God. Paul says that the moment you believe with your heart on the Lord Jesus, you are no longer strangers and aliens. You are full-fledged citizens in the Kingdom of God, acquainted with the ways of the King and the heart of the King. You experience the benefits of all He did through His sinless life, His sacrificial death, and His bodily resurrection from the grave.

Are you a stranger and an alien? Paul says that if you are in Jesus, you are no longer strangers and aliens but fellow citizens with the saints. If you are in Jesus, you are a citizen. A citizen belongs to a kingdom. If you are in Jesus, you are in a new kingdom. You've changed your citizenship, and you are now under another authority. Being a citizen carries rights and privileges. But citizenship also means you have responsibilities; it means you are under authority.

> To be a citizen of the Kingdom of God means you are under the authority of King Jesus.

That is the first mark of citizenship.

The Bible recognizes two kingdoms in this world. There is the kingdom of this world characterized by death and darkness.

There is the Kingdom of God characterized by life and light. Every man and woman belongs to one of those kingdoms. Each man and woman is living either under the authority of Satan or the authority of God. One or the other has ultimate dominion over their lives. When you become a Christian, you move out of the kingdom of death and darkness, out from under the authority of Satan, and into the kingdom of light and life under the authority of Jesus. That is a radical change. That's what it means to be a Christian.

There is a radical and fundamental change of government. Jesus becomes the King of your life, the King of your heart. We are citizens of His Kingdom even while we are citizens of this country. "But our citizenship is in heaven, and from it we await a Savior, the Lord Jesus Christ" (Phil. 3:20). As citizens of the Kingdom of Jesus, we make decisions based on the concerns of our King. No matter where Christians live in this world, the concerns of Jesus become their concerns. In fact, they seek the concerns of their King and His Kingdom first and foremost.

> *Therefore do not be anxious, saying, "What shall we eat?" or "What shall we drink?" or "What shall we wear?" For the Gentiles seek after all these things, and your heavenly Father knows that you need them all. But seek first the kingdom of God and his righteousness, and all these things will be added to you.*
> —Matt. 6:31–33

> *For I have chosen him, that he may command his children and his household after him to keep the way of the LORD by doing righteousness and justice, so that the LORD may bring to Abraham what he has promised him.*
> —Gen. 18:19

He has told you, O man, what is good; and what does the LORD require of you but to do justice, and to love kindness, and to walk humbly with your God?
—Mic. 6:8

The man or woman who is a citizen in the Kingdom of God should be more concerned with human rights, social justice, and compassion than any citizen of any country in the world because our King is the author of humanity, our King is perfectly just, and our King is full of compassion. And while we are about our King's business, we should be humble about whatever it is we do for Him.

Living as citizens of God's Kingdom in this world will bring us into direct conflict with the values of fallen culture and in direct conflict with the god of this world. But we are promised the protection of the King. His power—resurrection power—the kind of power that works beyond human thinking and planning, is available to every citizen in His Kingdom. The King invites you to call on Him for His resources and His deliverance whenever you need them.

Here's the most amazing thing about being a fellow citizen in the Kingdom of God, and it is so amazing that it deserves the adjective "glorious." Our King is with us in this world. The King of our Kingdom walks with us. Our King is Emmanuel—God with us. Look at Him in the Gospels. He was with men and women in their greatest joys (we find Him at a wedding). He was with men and women in their deepest sorrows (we find Him at three funerals). He was with men and women when they were sick and needy. Unlike the kingdoms of man, our King tells us what's in His heart, tells us what moves Him to do what He does, and tells us the very end to which He is directing all of human history, as well as many of the details of how it's going to roll out.

How utterly mind-blowing is all of that? The implications are life-changing. We process every part of every day in light of the fact that because of Jesus we are no longer strangers and aliens. We process every part of every day in light of the fact that because of Jesus we are fellow citizens in His Kingdom. Whatever is going down in the world, no matter how bleak it looks, we can still have peace, joy, and hope.

I don't say this in a condescending way at all, but look at those whose lives are anchored in this present world, whose hopes rise and fall with politicians and political ideology. They are crushed when their candidate loses or their legislation fails. They have to demonize their opponents and accuse them as being unsophisticated and morally inferior. Go all the way back to the Christians living under the rule of the Roman emperor Nero, a violent, perverse lunatic, and you'll see something radical. The Christians just kept living as citizens of another Kingdom. No matter what goes down in the kingdoms of this world, we know that our King is still on the throne. We know that His Kingdom is the ultimate Kingdom and that His kingdom will ultimately win.

> *The kingdom of the world has become the kingdom of our Lord and of his Christ, and he shall reign forever and ever.*
>
> —Rev. 11:15

The Image of a Family

> *So then [consequently, as a consequence of being in Jesus] you are no longer strangers and aliens, but you are fellow citizens with the saints and members of the household of God.*
>
> —Eph. 2:19

As hard as it is to get our heads around this, the language is an advance on the language of kingdom and citizenship. If you are in Jesus, you are a member of God's own intimate family. Even as a very old man, the Apostle John couldn't get over how amazing that is.

Behold, what manner of love the Father has bestowed
on us, that we should be called children of God.
—1 John 3:1 NKJV

We are children of the living God! As great as it is to be a citizen, this is an advance. Citizenship is a legal relationship; family is a living relationship. A child always outranks any ambassador, governor, secretary, minister, or senator. A biography of Abraham Lincoln related an incident that occurred during the Civil War. Lincoln was involved with his cabinet in a very crucial meeting. While Lincoln and his cabinet were slogging out a strategy, there was a knock at the door. Lincoln's 10-year-old son was at the door. Lincoln dropped the most pressing duties of state and walked out on his cabinet members to see what his little boy needed. Lincoln's son outranked the president's cabinet and trumped the concerns of the Civil War.

If you have believed with your heart on the Lord Jesus Christ, then the God who was and is and is to come, who made everything out of nothing, who knows the number of the stars and calls them by name, who controls all things, is your Father. Here's what Jesus said to Mary Magdalene on the morning He conquered the grave: "I am ascending to my Father and your Father" (John 20:17).

There is nothing about your life that is too small or trivial. God is interested in every minute detail of your life because Jesus bought you. Unlike Lincoln, God doesn't have to stop running the universe to take care of His kids. He is the ultimate multitasker.

He listens to you and wipes away your tears. You get His undivided attention. That is what this doctrine means.

If you are in Jesus, God is your Father. Jesus is the only way anyone can ever have that relationship. I have to roll back to verse 18 here. "For through him we both have access in one Spirit to the Father."

The word *access* is *prosagōge*. It had to do with privileged entrance or access. There were those in the ancient world who were given the title *prosagōgos*. Their job was to take someone and introduce them to the king. So when we look at this word, we want to think of more than privileged entrance. We want to think of proper introduction. Paul wants us to know that we have been properly introduced to God the Father. That is what Jesus has done for us.

J. B. Phillips tells the story of a little boy who walked up to the gate at Buckingham Palace and kept saying to one of the guards, "I want to see the king! I want to see the king." While the little boy kept saying that, a man in a suit walked up behind the little boy. The man took the little boy by the hand and walked him into the entrance of Buckingham Palace. He walked the boy down a corridor with 40 rooms along it. In one of those rooms was a dining room with a table the size of an ice rink. The man led the boy past room after room and then up to the second floor. They finally came to a room that was a quarter of a mile from where they entered the palace. The man in the suit knocked on the door. The door opened, and there stood the King of England. There was the little boy holding the hand of the man in the suit. The man in the suit was Prince Phillip, the son of the king. He said, "Dad, this is Willy. I found him out front. He said he wanted to meet you." Willy and the king had a conversation that day.

That's what's wrapped up in the word *access*. The Son has taken us by the hand and led us to His Father. In Jesus, with Jesus, by Jesus, and through Jesus we have access we could have never experienced. Jesus said, "I am the way, and the truth, and the life. No one comes to the Father except through me" (John 14:6).

Jesus doesn't just gain us access and formal introduction to God as privileged guests.

> *But to all who did receive him, who believed in his name, he gave the right to become children of God, who were born, not of blood nor of the will of the flesh nor of the will of man, but of God.*
>
> —John 1:12–13

The very nature of authentic Christianity is inextricably tied to this. A Christian is someone who by virtue of the new birth is a child of God—period. You cannot be a Christian without being a child of God, and you can't be a child of God without being born again.

The witness of the church in the world is significantly tied to this. On the human level, children share in the genetic nature of their parents. The authentic Christian is someone born of God, and as a child of God, they are "partakers of the divine nature" (2 Pet. 1:4). The church is not a bunch of people doing their best to behave or trying their best to act like God. The church is a group of people who are partaking of the nature of God. They have the Holy Spirit living in them, imparting to them, and forming in them the character of God.

Paul already introduced us to this at the beginning of his letter where he said that God "predestined us for adoption to himself as sons through Jesus Christ, according to the purpose of his will" (Eph. 1:5). Now Paul wants to press upon our hearts the radical privilege of being children of the living God. God is our Father. We can go to the everlasting and eternal God as our Father. Jesus said, "I am ascending to my Father and your Father" (John 20:17).

The privilege of being a child of the living God gets even more amazing!

> *For all who are led by the Spirit of God are sons of God. For you did not receive the spirit of slavery to fall back into fear, but you have received the Spirit of adoption as sons, by whom we cry, "Abba! Father!" The Spirit himself bears witness with our spirit that we are children of God, and if children, then heirs—heirs of God and fellow heirs with Christ.*
>
> —Rom. 8:14–17

If you are in Jesus, that is the truth about you. Whatever your socioeconomic position may be, you are an heir of God. What does that mean? It is something so glorious that the Bible says very little about it. Our finite minds can't grasp it, and our finite language can't describe it. All we are told is that we will be with Jesus, and we will be like Jesus. We get thumbnail sketches of heaven in the book of Revelation, and what awaits us is infinitely greater than that.

> *Blessed are the pure in heart, for they shall see God.*
>
> —Matt. 5:8

> *Blessed are the meek, for they shall inherit the earth.*
>
> —Matt. 5:5

> *According to his promise we are waiting for new heavens and a new earth in which righteousness dwells.*
>
> —2 Pet. 3:13

And do you remember where Paul was when He wrote this? He was in *prison*! Here's what Paul wrote to Timothy from prison:

If we suffer, we shall also reign with him.
—2 Tim. 2:12 KJV

Fix this picture firmly in your mind: Jesus, descended from the line of David, raised from the dead. It's what you've heard from me all along. It's what I'm sitting in jail for right now—but God's Word isn't in jail! That's why I stick it out here—so that everyone God calls will get in on the salvation of Christ in all its glory. This is a sure thing: If we die with him, we'll live with him; if we stick it out with him, we'll rule with him.
—2 Tim. 2:9–12 MSG

The Image of a Building

So then you are no longer strangers and aliens, but you are fellow citizens with the saints and members of the household of God, built on the foundation of the apostles and prophets, Christ Jesus himself being the cornerstone, in whom the whole structure, being joined together, grows into a holy temple in the Lord. In Him you also are being built together into a dwelling place for God by the Spirit
—Eph. 2:19-22

By inspiration of the Holy Spirit Paul tells us that God is building something out of this new humanity. Individually, we are building blocks in a living structure that is His dwelling place on this earth. That means that the Creator and King of the universe penetrates our lives and comes into us. There is nothing higher than that.

First, God is building a structure.

You are coming to Christ, who is the living cornerstone of God's temple. He was rejected by people, but he was chosen by God for great honor. And you are living stones that God is building into his spiritual temple.

—1 Pet. 2:4–5 NLT

How do you become a building block in this living structure? In the physical world, these building blocks have to be quarried. That metaphor explains what Jesus came to do. He is in the business of cutting stones out of the quarry of this fallen world.

I am a building block. This is amazing! We have been saved to be a building block. We were saved to fit into this amazing, supernatural collection of men and women who make up this thing called the church. We used to think that we could only find our deepest sense of meaning by being free-standing stones— our own buildings. Then we sought to foster and defend that identity by trying to fit in with other people who were trying to be free-standing stones in the same way we were trying to be free-standing stones. It's as if various tribes within a culture have their own uniforms, and everyone is just trying to fit in.

Tim Keller talks about a book he found that was written about Greenwich Village in New York. It had a section on the East Village, and at the end of that section it said, "How to look like you live in the East Village." Then there was a place about SoHo that said, "How to look like you live in SoHo." We were slaves to the hopelessly empty identity of being a free-standing stone, trying desperately to fit in with other free-standing stones in the hope of finding an ultimate meaning in life. The gospel says our desire for ultimate meaning is finally satisfied when we, by the grace of God, fit in and have our place in this living structure we call the church.

As we look at this supernatural structure, we see foundation, formation, and function. We need to let each of these examine us individually as a unique building block in this structure and then examine us corporately as a local church.

1. *Foundation*

In the realm of architecture, a building block has to be related to the foundation. Everyone is building their lives on some kind of foundation. Every man or woman in Jesus is a building block that must be built on the foundation supplied by God. Ephesians 1:20 says we are "built on the foundation of the apostles and prophets." This is so significant! This structure God is building demands a foundation that never changes and never shifts.

Foundation = *bdag* (Greek-English Lexicon): the structural base for a building; the indispensable prerequisites for something to come into being

The foundation for this living temple was laid by the apostles and the New Testament prophets. The apostles examined Jesus nearly every moment for more than two years. They heard Him speak, heard the way He spoke, and saw the look in His eyes when He spoke. Jesus explained to them the things He said. They heard and also saw all Jesus did and the way He lived. They were convinced that Jesus was God in human flesh.

> *That which was from the beginning, which we have heard, which we have seen with our eyes, which we looked upon and have touched with our hands, concerning the word of life—the life was made manifest, and we have seen it, and testify to it and proclaim to you the eternal life, which was with the Father and was made manifest to us that which we have seen and heard we proclaim also to you, so that you too may*

*have fellowship with us; and indeed our fellowship is
with the Father and with his Son Jesus Christ.*

—1 John 1:1–3

The faith of the first Christians was built on the testimony and teaching of those men. "They devoted themselves to the apostles' teaching" (Acts 2:42). And we build our lives on what they believed and taught about Jesus. "The faith that was once for all delivered to the saints" (Jude 1:3). Paul spoke of himself as "a skilled master builder" who "laid a foundation" (1 Cor. 3:10).

The foundation for what God is building has been laid securely and irrevocably. That foundation is the inspired, inerrant Word of God, the changeless truth that is all about Jesus who *is* the foundation. "For no one can lay a foundation other than that which is laid, which is Jesus Christ" (1 Cor. 3:11). A working definition of Inerrancy: "When all the facts are known, the Bible (in it's original writings) properly interpreted in light of which culture and communication means had developed by the time of its composition will be shown to be completely true (and therefore not false) in all that it affirms, to the degree of precision intended by the author, in all matters relating to God and His creation."[22]

*Everyone then who hears these words of mine and
does them will be like a wise man who built his house
on the rock. And the rain fell, and the floods came,
and the winds blew and beat on that house, but it did
not fall, because it had been founded on the rock. And
everyone who hears these words of mine and does not
do them will be like a foolish man who built his house*

---

22. David S. Dockery; Christian Scripture: An Evangelical Perspective on Inspiration, Authority, and Interpretation [Nashville: Broadman & Holman, 1995], 64

*on the sand. And the rain fell, and the floods came,
and the winds blew and beat against that house, and
it fell, and great was the fall of it.*

—Matt. 7:24–27

The building block is *not* the foundation. But there are a lot of professing Christians who have taken it upon themselves to redefine the foundation that the church stands on. They say, "Hey, there's a lot of good stuff in the Bible, but surely we can't look at the Bible the way Christians looked at it 50 years ago. There are simply parts of the Bible that we can't accept anymore." They make themselves the final authority on the Bible rather than letting the Bible be the final authority on them. They've decided that they will be the foundation instead of being the building blocks. They're saying, "My own mind and my own heart are going to be the foundation."

When that happens there's no longer an unshifting, changeless foundation. Think about it. How are you going to decide what is right and wrong? Science can't help. Science can only tell us what is. It can never tell us what ought to be. Are you going to look at your own heart to define your foundation? A week ago, a year ago, a decade ago you were playing the fool. How do you know you're not playing the fool now? Are you going to look at fallen culture to determine ultimate values and morality, to see what the masses have to say? That is how we used to live, right? (Eph. 2:1–3). Fallen culture is tragically trapped in chronological arrogance. The culture of the moment looks down on the preceding generation(s). They say that the moral values of 100 years ago were so wrong, even despicable. But here's the trap. How do you know that years from now people won't be looking at the belief system you pride yourself in today and say, "How could anybody have believed that?"

When building blocks decide to be the foundation, they undermine the basis for the supernatural unity or, in architectural language, the structural integrity of this living structure from which and through which God puts the glory of Jesus on display in this world.

Are you a building block trying to be the foundation? Is your opinion the foundation by which you judge Scripture, or is Scripture the foundation by which you judge your opinion? Every building block is built on the unshakable foundation of the Word of God, on the unchanging truth of who Jesus is and all He has done. The one who is the subject and centerpiece of the Word is "Christ Jesus himself being the cornerstone" (Eph. 2:20). "You are coming to Christ, who is the living cornerstone of God's temple" (1 Pet. 2:4 NLT). The cornerstone functioned as the stone that oriented all other stones—the stone that unified the entire building.

The Pulpit Commentaries has this note on the cornerstone:

> The stone which, being placed in the corner, determined the lines of the whole building. The idea of foundation is that of support; the idea of the chief cornerstone is that of regulation, pattern-hood, producing assimilation. Jesus is not only the Origin, Foundation, Support of the Church, but he gives it its shape and form, he determines the place and the office of each stone, he gives life and character to each member.[23]

Martyn Lloyd-Jones said, "Everyone who is truly a member of the Christian Church is not only related to the faith of the

23. Henry D. M. Spence-Jones, Ed., *Ephesians* (London: Funk & Wagnalls, 1909), 67.

apostles, he is also in a very definite relationship to the Lord Jesus Christ Himself.[24]

Here's the picture. Remember, every measurement of a building is taken from the cornerstone. The whole building ties together because of the cornerstone. That is who Jesus is to every authentic Christian. Paul constantly and consistently tied every aspect of our new identity to Jesus. Charles Spurgeon said, "The Christian life is begun, continued, and perfected altogether in connection with the Lord Jesus Christ."[25]

Everything is in Christ, in Him, by Him, through Him, through His blood, and by His death. Paul doesn't want us for a moment to think of ourselves apart from Jesus. Peter refers to Jesus as "a cornerstone chosen and precious" (1 Pet. 2:6). He is infinitely precious—irreplaceable. Every stone in this living temple is measured by Him (I'm not measured by feeling or opinion; I'm not measured by other people). Every dimension of who I am in Jesus and where I fit in His body is always in reference to Jesus. He sets the standard. He is the first stone that was laid. He is the one who gives us our new identity. Every stone in this living temple is being conformed to the image of Christ Jesus. Everything about the house of God is governed by Jesus. All the growth, all the unity, and everything about this living temple depend on the cornerstone.

Jesus is the great cornerstone of every living stone in this living structure. We are joined to Him, and we find our place in the building relative to Him. When we calibrate our lives relative to the Chief Cornerstone, we are never out of place. We are exactly

---

24. Martyn Lloyd-Jones, *God's Way of Reconciliation: An Exposition of Ephesians 2* (Grand Rapids, MI: Baker Books), 360.
25. Charles Haddon Spurgeon, *Sermons of the Rev. C. H. Spurgeon, of London, Volume 23*, Google Books, 37.

where we should be in this living temple, surrounded by exactly the other building blocks He wants us to be joined to. And when Jesus is the reference point, when every living stone is in that kind living relationship to Jesus, the presence of the Holy Spirit overshadows the lack of ability to articulate the gospel or answer the objections, and people are drawn to Jesus.

2. *Formation*

> *Christ Jesus himself being the cornerstone, in whom the whole structure, being joined together, grows into a holy temple in the Lord. In him you also are being built together into a dwelling place for God by the Spirit.*
>
> —Eph. 2:20–22

Look at the words *in whom.* Jesus is the agent, the one who accomplishes everything that is said about this living habitation of God. The joining together of each living stone and the growth of this structure happens in union with Him.

Now look at the words *joined together,* which literally means "fit together in a coherent and compatible manner." It is translated from a compound Greek word. The prefix is *syn* (pronounced soon), which is the preposition "with." *Syn* expresses intimate union. It tells us that as building blocks, we're not merely together with one another but so fitted together that you can't tell where one living stone ends and another one begins. We are so with, so fitted, that we can't get apart from each other. I like an illustration for this that has to do with food. Does anyone like biscuits? You can take all the ingredients and put them on the countertop. All those ingredients are *with* each other, but you can't use *syn* to describe their togetherness. You would use the Greek preposition *meta* because although they are together, they are still separate. But take all those ingredients and mix them together, put them in a pan, and put them in the oven. After a while, they come out as an amazing union of ingredients—*syn*—that can't be separated.

There are two more things about being joined together. First, the process of being joined together is an ongoing process. It begins at the moment of conversion and continues until the day we see Jesus face to face. Remember, Jesus is the agent. He started all this. He saved us and quarried us out. He is the one who is shaping and fitting and placing us. Paul told the Philippians that he was confident that Jesus would complete His work in each living stone. "And I am sure of this, that he who began a good work in you will bring it to completion at the day of Jesus Christ" (Phil. 1:6).

He said the same thing to the Thessalonian believers. "He who calls you is faithful; he will surely do it" (1 Thess. 5:24). Jesus quarries, fits, and finishes each block.

Second, being joined together is in the passive voice—something is being done to us. The unity and symmetry of this living house of God is the result of every living stone being fitted—being joined together.

Every living stone has a specific place in the building, and they are being shaped and fitted for the place they occupy. They are handpicked for the place they occupy in the whole of the building and in relationship to the other living stones around them. They are not only handpicked but they are handcrafted for the part they play in the whole of the building and in their relationship to the living stones they are surrounded by.

Both Jew and Gentile fully got the picture. For the Gentile converts of Ephesus before they came to faith in Jesus, the temple of Diana was a source of tremendous pride. The Jews who had come to faith in Jesus knew from their own history the craftsmanship in the construction of Solomon's temple, how each stone was quarried and then hand-shaped by master craftsmen to fit so perfectly that no mortar was required and the tolerances so small that you couldn't slip a paper knife between the stones. Each stone was numbered, which means it was quarried and shaped for a place to fit with very specific stones. And all of them were oriented to the cornerstone.

Our fitting is something done to us by God. Yet the stones in this structure are not like the lifeless components of a lifeless structure that has no feelings. Peter said that Christians are "living stones." We need to remember that the building block is not the foundation nor is the building block the architect. As living stones, we must be willing to allow the Master Architect to shape us, place us, and fit us as He desires.

Are you going to let God fit you, or are you going to fight Him? In Solomon's quarry, the stone didn't get to choose the chisel or the shape or the place it would occupy. All of that was determined by the wisdom of the chief architect. God is the Chief Architect of this living temple. He makes every living stone exactly what He wants them to be. God uses different tools in our life to do that shaping that will fit us perfectly for the place and part we play.

We might not like the way God is shaping us, but if we knew what He was shaping us for, we would fully agree that His design is perfect. Everything going on in our life is part of the process. We might not like the tools He uses such as adversity, suffering, blessings, and relationships. Some tools are designed to knock off big chunks. They come at us with great force. Others do the fine finish work such as sanding and polishing, making the articulating surface of our life capable of tremendous unity. I believe that the chief instrument in shaping and defining our lives is the Word of God. It is alive and powerful. It can come at us like a wrecking ball, and it can perform microsurgery.

That divine formation leads to function "in whom the whole structure, being joined together, grows into a holy temple in the Lord" (Eph. 2:21).

A holy temple – The normal word for temple means the whole complex, all the precincts of the temple. The word Paul uses here does not describe the whole temple complex. He uses the word that describes the Holy of Holies. It was in the Holy of Holies where God met with His people.

Because of what Jesus did to save us, our bodies are now the temple of the Holy Spirit. Every living stone is the dwelling place of God.

> *Or do you not know that your body is a temple [naos = Holy of Holies] of the Holy Spirit within you, whom you have from God? You are not your own, for you were bought with a price. So glorify God in your body.*
> —1 Cor. 6:19–20

God is taking every living stone, each indwelled by the Holy Spirit, and is building them into a living temple that is at this very moment growing. "Do you [plural, speaks of all believers collectively and so of the church] not know that you are God's temple and that God's Spirit dwells in you?" (1 Cor. 3:16). Paul was writing to a local church. This verse views the local church as the temple of God inhabited by His Spirit.

What is our purpose of being put into this temple? It is so God might indwell us, that God might commune with us, and that God might fellowship with us. God desires to fellowship with us, and He wants us to be the vessel on this earth that He indwells. He wants to meet with us. The local church is where God places us so we can meet Him, experience Him, and grow in grace and in the knowledge of Him. He is the architect. He wants to give us His design. He wants to empower us for His ministry and His work.

This living temple is growing. And the growth of this living temple and the growth of every individual building block is something only God can do. Man can fill buildings, but only God can grow this living temple and the stones that comprise it. It is continually undergoing construction. It is growing by addition. That is God's doing (see Acts 2 where the Lord added to the church). It is growing by maturation. That is the Lord's doing.

> *He handed out gifts of apostle, prophet, evangelist, and pastor-teacher to train Christ's followers in skilled servant work, working within Christ's body, the church, until we're all moving rhythmically and easily with each other, efficient and graceful in response to God's Son, fully mature adults, fully developed within and without, fully alive like Christ.*
>
> —Eph. 4:11–13 MSG

The formation is related to function. Every living building block is quarried, shaped, and placed for a specific purpose—growth. Paul writes more about this in Ephesians 4.

> *From whom the whole body, being fitted and held together by what every joint supplies, according to the proper working of each individual part, causes the growth of the body for the building up of itself in love.*
>
> —Eph. 4:16 NASB

Some have a low view of church. "Church is an option," they say. Paul is telling us that this new kind of humanity has been saved to and for *ekklesia*. Christianity is community. The individual Christian only finds their true place when they are built into the church, fitted with and connected to the other believers who make up this living structure.

When you are trying to live out your new identity in Jesus by yourself, you are attempting the impossible. God saved you, quarried you out to be a building block—a living stone—fitted alongside other living stones. To not be in accountable relationships with other Christians, to not bear one another's burdens and have other people bear your burdens is a violation of your new nature, an aberration of the new kind of humanity God is making in Jesus.

Elsewhere in the New Testament we're told how community is essential to this new kind of humanity. Christians are to submit to each out of reverence for Jesus (Eph. 5:21), confess their sins to each other (James 5:16), bear each other's burdens and thus fulfill the law of Christ (Gal. 6:2), exhort each other daily lest we be hardened by the deceitfulness of sin (Heb. 3:13), and think of ways to motivate one another to acts of love and good works, not neglecting meeting together but encourage one another, especially now that the day of His return is drawing near (Heb. 10:24–25).

This means that church is not an option. Every believer has a place in a community of other believers because that is the plan of the Architect. Others have a wrong view of church. For them, church is about what they take away, what church offers *them*. They connect with the church like consumers instead of like building blocks.

Here's the deal. All that I am in Jesus, all that I am by His workmanship, is inextricably tied to where He places me so I can be part of the growth of other believers who also become God's instrument in my growth. Church is not just about me; it's not just about you. There can be no gaps. They have to be built into each other.

Are you doing that? Are you continually widening your circle of people you have that kind of relationship with in the church? What God does in us together is important. He is building something out of us together. The local church is where God places us so we can meet Him, experience Him, and grow in grace and in the knowledge of Him.

I pray that we will be absolutely overwhelmed at how amazing our salvation is. We were once without God in the world. Now we are citizens in His Kingdom. We were once orphaned by our sin. Now we are members of His family. And we are His dwelling place!

chapter twelve

i am a steward of a sacred mystery

Ephesians 3:1–13

Ephesians 3 ends the first section of this incredible book of the Bible, which is actually a letter. The first three chapters tell us so much about the new and true identity of every man and woman who believes with their heart in the Lord Jesus.

> *For this reason I, Paul, a prisoner for Christ Jesus on behalf of you Gentiles—assuming that you have heard of the stewardship of God's grace that was given to me for you, how the mystery was made known to me by revelation, as I have written briefly. When you read this, you can perceive my insight into the mystery of Christ, which was not made known to the sons of men in other generations as it has now been revealed to his holy apostles and prophets by the Spirit. This mystery is that the Gentiles are fellow heirs, members of the*

*same body, and partakers of the promise in Christ
Jesus through the gospel. Of this gospel I was made
a minister according to the gift of God's grace, which
was given me by the working of his power. To me,
though I am the very least of all the saints, this grace
was given, to preach to the Gentiles the unsearchable
riches of Christ, and to bring to light for everyone
what is the plan of the mystery hidden for ages in God
who created all things, so that through the church the
manifold wisdom of God might now be made known
to the rulers and authorities in the heavenly places.
This was according to the eternal purpose that he has
realized in Christ Jesus our Lord, in whom we have
boldness and access with confidence through our faith
in him. So I ask you not to lose heart over what I am
suffering for you, which is your glory.*

—Eph. 3:1–13

This third chapter opens with Paul saying "for this reason."
He's going to continue to unpack and explain all God has done
for us in, with, by, and through Jesus. And the next element of
our rescue, the next element of who we are in Jesus, builds on and
flows out of what he has just said in Ephesians 1 and 2.

In Chapter 2, he framed the gospel in terms of circumcision
and uncircumcision so we might begin to understand how
transformational the gospel really is. He showed us that the gospel
is so powerful that it actually destroys the historic hostilities and
tears down the walls of hatred and bigotry that existed between
Jews and Gentiles. That horizontal reconciliation was the result of
vertical reconciliation. It is by reconciling the individual to Himself
that God tears down centuries of ancient hatred and bigotry that
was rooted in race, gender, culture, politics, and socioeconomics.

Paul tells us how God—through Jesus—is making a new kind of humanity of those two groups.

At the close of Ephesians 2, Paul described the outcome of our reconciliation in terms of three distinct figures. They build on each other, one on the previous one, each packed with truth about who we are in Jesus. In Ephesians 2:19 we see that we are "fellow citizens with the saints." Then we see in that same verse the figure of a family, "members of the household of God." Finally, we see the figure of a building in verses 21–22, "a holy temple in the Lord . . . being built together into a dwelling place for God by the Spirit."

We've looked closely at how every man and woman in Jesus is a building block. Paul spoke about that identity in terms of foundation, formation, and function. Now Paul starts the third chapter by saying, "For this reason I, Paul, a prisoner for Christ Jesus on behalf of you Gentiles." I think he was going to say, "For this reason I, Paul, a prisoner for Christ Jesus on behalf of you Gentiles bow my knees before the Father," but he made a sudden detour. I believe he did that because he was not only Paul the apostle, Paul the evangelist, and Paul the church planter who had planted the church in Ephesus, but he was also Paul the pastor.

He was writing to men and women he had pastored for three years. He's starting to pray for them, and as soon as he mentions the fact he's in prison, he stops. He doesn't dive into telling them what he is praying for them because he realizes that the men and women who are so dear to Jesus and so dear to him might be confused and discouraged by the fact he is in prison. So he takes the time to tell them *why* he is in prison.

As we look at this detour in his letter, we will learn more about who we are in Jesus. But we will also learn (and I think this is a big reason for Paul's digression) that there is something we are not.

I am in Christ — I am a saint — I am blessed.
I am chosen — I am holy — I am without blame.
I am loved — I am adopted — I am accepted.
I am redeemed — I am forgiven — I am safe in the plan
of God.
I am sealed by the Holy Spirit — I am alive in God.
I am His workmanship — I am reconciled.
I am a citizen — I am a child of God — I am a building
block.

. . . But I am not free from suffering!

Who we are in Jesus does not exempt us from suffering in a broken world. But Paul also wants us to understand that bad things happen to us because of who we are in Jesus.

Twice in this letter Paul told the Christians in Ephesus (and us) that he was a prisoner (Eph. 3:1, 4:1). At the end of his letter, he refers to himself as "an ambassador in chains" (Eph. 6:20). Paul wanted them (and us) to know that he was in prison because he was telling people about Jesus.

Think about it. Aren't you forever thankful for the person(s) who led you to faith in Jesus? You should be! Everything you have in your relationship with God is because someone loved Jesus and loved you enough to tell you about Jesus. But now imagine that same person telling you that they are in prison for doing the very thing they did in leading you to faith in Jesus. Paul makes this detour to give context and clarity to his suffering.

By way of this divinely inspired detour, Paul tells us that when our lives are consistent with the gospel we proclaim, the more likely we are to suffer for Christ. You can suffer socially and emotionally because you allow Jesus to define your sexuality and your sexual behavior. You can suffer socially, academically, and professionally if you stand up and identify yourself as a Christian.

You can suffer socially, financially, and professionally if you allow Jesus to define your business ethics.

There's another sphere in which we can experience adversity and suffering. Think about the text in Luke 10 and what it means to love your neighbor as yourself. In the story of the Good Samaritan, Jesus made it clear that we have a very short list of who our neighbor is. We think of our neighbor as the person who is most like us, people we like, people who like us, or people who agree with us. But the hero of the story risked his life and opened his wallet to save a man who had nothing in common with him. In fact, the man he was helping was on the opposite side of an ethnic and religious culture war that had existed for hundreds of years. That hit me like a wrecking ball! That means we're to love in tangible ways people who reject and resent the gospel, people who reject and resent us for telling them about the gospel, people who reject and resent us for the way we seek to live consistently with the teaching of Scripture. You know who might persecute you for living that way? Other Christians! You might say, "How can you actually sit down with that person? How can you actually love and help that person? They voted for _____, they're involved in a same-sex relationship, they're pro-abortion!"

Our lives are supposed to be consistent with what we believe. Our lives are supposed to be consistent with the grace we've experienced in Jesus. Paul is going to spend the next huge chunk of this letter telling us that who we are in Jesus defines how we live for Jesus in a world that is living without Jesus and against Jesus. If we live in a way that is consistent with the gospel, it is inevitable that we will face adversity, hardship, and suffering. Jesus said this same thing the night before He died for our sins. "I have said these things to you, that in me you may have peace. In the world you will have tribulation. But take heart; I have overcome the world" (John 16:33).

Paul is going to explain to his readers (that includes you and me) that he looks at his circumstances in light of who he is in Jesus.

> *Assuming that you have heard of the stewardship of God's grace that was given to me for you, how the mystery was made known to me by revelation, as I have written briefly. When you read this, you can perceive my insight into the mystery of Christ, which was not made known to the sons of men in other generations as it has now been revealed to his holy apostles and prophets by the Spirit.*
>
> —Eph. 3:2–5

There are two big words here: *stewardship* and *mystery*. Let's start with the word *mystery*. In the Bible, a mystery is not something to be figured out. It's not like a great drama where you observe all the characters, piece together all the evidence, and come p with the who-done-it. In the Bible, mystery has to do with the truth concerning God and His dealings with mankind that are unknown to them and unknowable by them unless and until it is unfolded and revealed by God.

Deuteronomy 29:29 speaks directly to this: "The secret things belong to the LORD our God, but the things that are revealed belong to us and to our children forever." That is exactly what Paul says in Ephesians 3:4–5 about "the mystery of Christ, which was not made known to the sons of men in other generations as it has now been revealed."

Paul spoke to that when he said in 1 Corinthians 1:21 that "the world did not know God through wisdom." That is so crucial for us to understand. Apart from God revealing Himself to mankind, every effort of philosophers and religious leaders to discover God has been mere speculation—finite people starting from finite and fallen wisdom and trying to discover the infinite God. In utter contrast to that, revelation is God reaching down to fallen and finite people who were hopelessly groping in the dark for God. Martyn Lloyd-Jones said, "We must start by laying down this postulate: our only hope of knowing God truly is that He should be graciously pleased to reveal Himself to us, and the Christian teaching is that God has done that."[26]

By the way, the Bible is not incidental to being a Christian. There are men and women who say they love Jesus but don't really like the Bible. Well, who is this Jesus they love? Is He the Jesus of their own invention? Why do they love this Jesus? What is it about Jesus that makes them love Him? How do they grow in their love for Jesus? Peter said, "Grow in the grace and knowledge of our Lord and Savior Jesus Christ" (2 Pet. 3:18). Jesus said on more than one occasion that the Bible is all about Him.

Let's get back to this mystery. What is it that at one time was unknown and unknowable to mankind? The New Living Translation is really helpful here.

> As you read what I have written, you will understand my insight into this plan regarding Christ. God did not reveal it to previous generations, but now by His Spirit he has revealed it to his holy apostles and prophets. And this is God's plan: Both Gentiles and Jews who believe the Good News share equally in the riches inherited by God's children.
>
> —Eph. 3:4–6 NLT

---

26. James Lau, "The Doctrine of Revelation of God by Martyn Lloyd Jones," *My Inward Journey*, October 5, 2020, https://jameslau88.com/2020/05/10/the-doctrine-of-revelation-of-god-by-martyn-lloyd-jones/.

First, Paul wants us to know this wasn't his invention.

Second, God had this sacred secret in mind all along. It wasn't an afterthought. And it was still a sacred secret even at the beginning of the book of Acts. *The Bible Knowledge Commentary* states, "The mystery is not that Gentiles would be saved, for the Old Testament gave evidence of that, but rather that believing Jews and Gentiles are joined together. That was a revolutionary concept for Jews and Gentiles alike!"[27]

This sacred secret doesn't hit us like it would have hit the church in the first century because we live a long way down the road of history, and we live for the most part in a very non-Jewish world. But it was absolutely earth-shattering news in first century Christianity to be told that believing Jews and believing Gentiles were joined together into one body, that Jews and Gentiles were collectively the *ekklesia.*

> *As you read over what I have written to you, you'll be able to see for yourselves into the mystery of Christ. None of our ancestors understood this. Only in our time has it been made clear by God's Spirit through his holy apostles and prophets of this new order. The mystery is that people who have never heard of God and those who have heard of him all their lives (what I've been calling outsiders and insiders) stand on the same ground before God. They get the same offer, same help, same promises in Christ Jesus. The Message is accessible and welcoming to everyone, across the board.*
> —Eph. 3:4–6 MSG

---

27. H. W. Hoehner, "Ephesians," In John F. Walvoord and Roy B. Zuck, Eds., *The Bible Knowledge Commentary: An Exposition of the Scriptures, Volume 2,* (Wheaton, IL: Victor Books, 1985), 629.

Though we might not feel the impact of what Paul is saying in the same way Jews and Gentiles did in the early church, it should hit us really hard that through the gospel, all people have an equal standing in Jesus. It should hit us like a freight train that the gospel should be withheld from *no one*. The gospel is for *everyone*. The gospel should go *everywhere*!

Stewardship

Ephesians 3:2 says, "assuming that you have heard of the stewardship of God's grace that was given to me for you." This word *stewardship* comes from two Greek words: *oikos*, meaning "house," and *nomos*, meaning "law." We actually get our English word *economy* from the Greek *oikonomia*, which means "the law of the house" or "a stewardship, a management."

At the time Paul wrote this letter, the steward was a man entrusted with the privilege and responsibility of dispensing and dispersing the wealth and assets of the master of the house. The treasures did not belong to the steward, but he was responsible for using his master's treasures as the master directed him.

Don't miss this! Here is the *economy* of the gospel: in Jesus we are *stewards*. God gives us the treasures of the gospel for others.

From the moment Paul surrendered his life to Jesus on the road to Damascus, God made it clear that Paul was to bring the good news concerning Jesus to the Gentiles (Acts 9:15, 26:13–18). He was a faithful steward of the message of the gospel and of this sacred secret that God made known to him. Wherever Paul went he planted local churches that were made up of believing Jews and Gentiles. Here's what he wrote to the Christians in Galatia:

> For in Christ Jesus you are all sons of God, through faith. For as many of you as were baptized into Christ have put on Christ. There is neither Jew nor Greek, there is neither

slave nor free, there is no male and female, for you are all one in Christ Jesus. And if you are Christ's, then you are Abraham's offspring, heirs according to promise.

—Gal. 3:26–29

For his faithful stewardship in that sacred secret, Paul was constantly under attack by unbelieving Jews and even believing Jews. But he was so clear about this sacred secret of the Jews and Gentiles being united in Jesus that he went out of his way to collect an offering among the predominantly Gentile churches he had planted to bring aid to the suffering church in Jerusalem that was made up primarily of Jews who had trusted Christ. He even brought the gift in person (Acts 21:17–19).

But while Paul was in Jerusalem, he was violently assaulted on the temple mount. He defended himself by giving his personal testimony. The crowd was totally engaged until he said one word—*Gentiles!* That word ignited a riot. The rest of the book of Acts explains how Paul went from Jerusalem to Rome, not as a free man proclaiming the gospel but as a prisoner, all because he had been a faithful steward. He was faithful to proclaim the good news of salvation through Christ. He was faithful to proclaim how faith in Jesus not only reconciles the individual to God but reconciles Jews and Gentiles to each other. And by faith in Jesus, Jews and Gentiles become one in Christ.

Here's the point. If you are a Christian, it is because you have personally heard and believed the gospel. You live in the reality of this sacred secret. It doesn't matter if before coming to Jesus you were ethnically Jewish or non-Jewish, religious or irreligious, moral or immoral. Because you are *in Jesus*, you have equal standing alongside all who have believed with their hearts on the Lord Jesus. All of us stand before God on the ground of grace, this grace on which we stand.

Everyone who is *in Jesus* has equal standing in grace and the privilege of being stewards of grace. Everyone who is *in Jesus* has access to the same power of God that enabled Paul to be a faithful steward of God's grace. But the outcome of this sacred secret doesn't stop there. "Of this gospel I was made a minister according to the gift of God's grace, which was given me by the working of his power" (Eph. 3:7).

The word *working* is *energeia* from which we get our word *energy*. The word *power* is *dunamis*, which gives us our words *dynamic* and *dynamite*. Paul's faithful stewardship of the message of the gospel was not due to his intellectual power, his physical power, or his emotional power. Instead, his emotional, physical, and intellectual abilities were energized by the power of God.

And the outcome of this sacred secret doesn't stop even here. Everyone who is *in Jesus* has access to "the unsearchable riches of Christ" (Eph. 3:8). Charles Spurgeon put it this way: "I am bold to tell you that my Master's riches of grace are so unsearchable, that he delights to forgive and forget enormous sin; the bigger the sin the more glory to his grace. If you are over head and ears in debt, he is rich enough to discharge your liabilities. If you are at the very gates of hell, he is able to pluck you from the jaws of destruction."[28]

Do you need peace? The peace of Jesus passes understanding. Do you need love? The love of Christ is beyond understanding.

The depths of the life, love, grace, mercy, compassion, and peace that belong to the believer in Jesus are too great to be measured. Some translate *unsearchable* as "untraceable"—so vast you cannot discover the end.

---

28. Charles Haddon Spurgeon, "A Grateful Summary of Twenty Volumes," *The Spurgeon Center*, December 27, 1874.

What is God going to do through this sacred secret He has made known? Look again at Ephesians 3:9–12:

> *And to bring to light for everyone what is the plan of the mystery hidden for ages in God who created all things, so that through the church the manifold wisdom of God might now be made known to the rulers and authorities in the heavenly places. This was according to the eternal purpose that he has realized in Christ Jesus our Lord, in whom we have boldness and access with confidence through our faith in him.*

Did you notice that phrase "through the church the manifold wisdom of God"?

manifold wisdom = brilliant wisdom – the divine brilliance of the plan of redeeming our fallen world.

And after that is the phrase "might now be made known." Dean Alford points out that the words "might be made known" are emphatic, strongly contrasting the idea of *hidden* in verse 9. Writing on this, F. F. Bruce said, "The church thus appears to be God's pilot scheme for the reconciled universe of the future."[29] Wow! We are God's pilot plant for the reconciled universe of the future. Bruce went on to say, "The church, therefore, is to be a new society, not just a fellowship, a new society in which this world can see exhibited what family life, what business and economic practices, what race relations, what all of life will be under the healing kingship of Jesus Christ."

And it's not just for the world to see but also for "the rulers and authorities in the heavenly realms." Is that not just massive and amazing?

---

29. F. F. Bruce, *The Epistles to the Colossians, to Philemon, and to the Ephesians* (Grand Rapids, MI: Eerdmans, 1984), 321–322.

chapter thirteen

now that you know who you are

Ephesians 3:14–21

In the first three chapters of this amazing letter, Paul has unpacked for us the outworking of all God has done for us through Jesus's virgin birth, sinless life, sacrificial death and bodily resurrection. We've seen that the gospel not only promises a new destiny for the man or woman who would believe with their heart on the Lord Jesus but also provides a new and true identity—the answer to "Who am I?"

The moment I believe the gospel, *I am* in Jesus. That means my life is totally and forever connected with Jesus. My life is forever and irrevocably identified with His life. Because I am in Jesus, I am a saint. Because I am in Jesus, I am blessed. Because I am in Jesus, I am chosen. Because I am in Jesus, I am holy. Because I am in Jesus, I am blameless. Because I am in Jesus, I am loved, adopted, and accepted. Because I am in Jesus, I am redeemed and forgiven. Because I am in Jesus, I am safe in the plan of God.

Because I am in Jesus, I am sealed by the Holy Spirit and alive to God. Because I am in Jesus, I am a citizen in the Kingdom of God, a child of God, and a building block in the church.

The second part of this amazing letter (Eph. 4:1–6:9) has to do with *how we live* for Jesus in a world living without Him. But Paul didn't start his letter there because the Christian life doesn't start there. How we live for Jesus flows from who we are in Jesus. Before Paul moves on to the second part of his letter, he writes his second prayer. If you remember, in the opening verse of Ephesians 3, Paul began to launch into that second prayer, but he took a divinely inspired detour and explained that in Jesus there is something we *are not*. We are *not* free from suffering!

Who we are in Jesus does not exempt us from suffering in a broken world. In fact, bad things can and will happen to us because of who we are in Jesus. In the middle of that divinely inspired detour, Paul tells us that every believer is a steward of a sacred secret—that through the gospel, all people have an equal standing in Jesus. "And this is God's plan: Both Gentiles and Jews who believe the Good News share equally in the riches inherited by God's children" (Eph. 3:6 NLT).

Finally, Paul gets to his second prayer.

> *For this reason I bow my knees before the Father, from whom every family in heaven and on earth is named, that according to the riches of his glory he may grant you to be strengthened with power through his Spirit in your inner being, so that Christ may dwell in your hearts through faith—that you, being rooted and grounded in love, may have strength to comprehend with all the saints what is the breadth and length and height and depth, and to know the love of Christ that surpasses knowledge, that you may be filled with*

*all the fullness of God. Now to him who is able to do
far more abundantly than all that we ask or think,
according to the power at work within us, to him be
glory in the church and in Christ Jesus throughout all
generations, forever and ever. Amen.*

—Eph. 3:14–21

We need to remember that this letter that stands as the Mount
Everest of the New Testament was written while Paul was in
prison. Paul wrote three letters from prison, and they contained
four prayers. They have one thing in common: they all deal with
the spiritual condition of the inner person. I find that so amazing
in light of the fact that he was in prison. Don't misunderstand
me; it isn't wrong to pray for physical and material needs. But
Paul, who knew a lot about suffering, also knew that life as God
intended it is not outside-in; it is inside-out. It is crucial that the
inner person be flourishing if we are going to navigate life between
the already and the not yet.

> Life in a broken world with bodies that are in the process of
> dying demand strength in the inner person.

That is no small bit of business. But here's the biggest thing
about this prayer. This second prayer deals with something that
is by and large foreign to the average believer and for many even
a bit frightening. Paul does *not* pray for the believers to merely
understand the amazing truth of all God has done for us *in Jesus,
with Jesus, by Jesus, and through Jesus.* He's not praying that the
Christians in Ephesus merely understand the concept of God's
adopting, accepting, redeeming love; he prays that they will have
a very real inner experience of that love. He is praying that they
will have a personal, experiential knowledge of Jesus.

J. Hudson Taylor prayed this every day: "Lord Jesus, make Thyself to me a living, bright reality."

It is the work of the Holy Spirit to not only reveal truth to our hearts but also to make Jesus a living, bright reality to us.

Let's walk through the last part of Ephesians 3 phrase by phrase. Verses 14–16 say, "For this reason I bow my knees before the Father, from whom every family in heaven and on earth is named, that according to the riches of his glory he may grant you to be strengthened with power through his Spirit in your inner being." It is your inner being where the Holy Spirit does this work that only He can do. He does it at the very center of who you are. It's one thing to know and trust the love of Christ, but it's another thing all together to actually experience these things at the very center of who you are.

Verse 17 says, "so that Christ may dwell in your hearts through faith." Then verse19 adds so you can "know the love of Christ that surpasses knowledge, that you may be filled with all the fullness of God."

Don't miss this! Paul is praying for things Christians already have. The New Testament repeatedly declares that by definition, a Christian is somebody in whom Christ dwells. Paul says it in Romans 8:10. Jesus said it in John 14:20 and 23. If Jesus doesn't dwell in you, you are not a Christian.

Here's what Paul wrote about Jesus to the Colossians: "For in him the whole fullness of deity dwells bodily, and you have been filled in him" (Col. 2:9–10). A Christian is someone who, from the moment they place their trust in Jesus alone to save them, has the fullness of God in them.

That begs the question that is key to understanding this prayer. Why would Paul pray for things that are already true of the Christian? A number of authors answer that question by way of this illustration: it's one thing to *have* a bank account; it's a different thing all together to *draw* on it.

For the sake of illustration, imagine that someone has paid off all your debts and then deposited $1 million into your bank account. The moment your debt was paid and that deposit entered into your account, you have a net worth of $1 million. You're rich! But it's one thing to have $1 million and another thing to draw on it. It's one thing to have $1 million and another thing to let it make an impact on the way you live, on the decisions you make, and on the people you're helping. Having $1 million is not the same as drawing it out.

The point of Paul's prayer is this: it's one thing to have God as your Father, Jesus as your loving Redeemer, your Brother, your King, and your Builder. But it's an all together different thing to experience God as your Father, Jesus as your loving Redeemer, Jesus as your Brother, Jesus as your King, and Jesus as your Builder.

Paul's prayer is recorded by inspiration of the Holy Spirit because God wants us to know that the heart of Paul in this prayer for the Ephesians is actually the heart of God for every Christian. It is God's heart that *you* will experience *the living, bright reality* of everything Jesus is.

We've already seen that someone is a Christian because Jesus has come to live in them. We don't always feel that, but by faith we live as though Jesus lives in our heart. That is God's immeasurable treasure deposited in the bank of your heart. Paul didn't pray that Christians would just understand that Jesus is there, that Christians would just know in a theological sense that Jesus is there. Paul prayed that Christians would experience the living, bright reality of His presence. He prayed "that Christ may dwell in your hearts through faith" (Eph. 3:17).

But Paul doesn't stop there. He not only prays for the Christian to experience the presence of Jesus; he prays for the

Christian to experience the living, bright reality of the love of Jesus. "That you, being rooted and grounded in love, may have strength to comprehend with all the saints what is the breadth and length and height and depth, and to know the love of Christ that surpasses knowledge" (Eph. 3:17–19).

But Paul doesn't stop even there! He not only prays for the Christian to experience the living, bright reality of the presence of Jesus and to experience the living, bright reality of the love of Jesus, but he prays for the Christian to experience the living, bright reality of the glory and greatness of God, "that you may be filled with all the fullness of God" (Eph. 3:19).

This is so heavy—literally! In the Old Testament, there are many references to the glory of God. The word *glory* means "weight." Paul is praying for them to experience the *fullness of God*, the glory, the weight, of God in such a way that God becomes infinitely more important than they ever thought possible, and that they experience God in such a way that everything they used to think was heavy now looks light.

It's one thing to know about the glory of God, the infinite weight and worth of God, but God has also revealed the truth of His glorious nature and attributes in the pages of Scripture. We live out every day of our life on this side of forever by trusting God to be everything He says about Himself in the Bible. Paul prayed that Christians would actually experience the weightiness—the glory—of God. Such an experience of the fullness of God leaves us utterly undone and humbled, yet absolutely fearless in the face of the heaviest trial or adversity.

> Experience His presence – verse 17
> Experience His love – verse 18
> Experience His glory – verse 19

There are biographies and autobiographies of men and women whose lives and words have been used by God in amazing and powerful ways. Let's look at what some of them have said in their own words about experiencing His presence, His love, and His glory. A lot of us have probably never experienced the things they have, but that's the reason we need to read about them. Think about the nature of what Paul got on his knees and prayed for. I pray their lives will show us what the Holy Spirit wants us to know about the presence of Jesus, the love of Jesus, and the fullness of God's glory.

Experience His presence:

> *He has unlocked every apartment of my being, and filled and flooded them all with the light of His radiant presence. . . . The spot before untouched has been reached, and all its flintiness has melted in the presence of that universal solvent, "Love divine, all loves excelling." . . . Jesus, the One altogether lovely.*[30]
>
> —Daniel Steele

Experience His love:

> *Well, one day, in the city of New York—oh, what a day!—I cannot describe it, I seldom refer to it; it is almost too sacred an experience to name. . . . I can only say that God revealed Himself to me, and I had*

---

30. "Reflection Guide: Ephesians 3:14–21," *Redemption Hill*, accessed February 27, 2022, https://redemptionhill.com/annyong/wp-content/uploads/2015/01/Ephesians3guide.pdf.

such an experience of His love that I had to ask Him to stay His hand.[31]
　　　　　　　　　　　　　　—Dwight L. Moody

The freeness and riches of God's everlasting love broke in with such light and power upon my soul, that I was often awed into silence and could not speak![32]
　　　　　　　　　　　　　　—George Whitefield

Some of us know at times what it is to be almost too happy to live! The love of God has been so overpoweringly experienced by us on some occasions, that we have almost had to ask for a stay of the delight because we could not endure any more.[33]
　　　　　　　　　　　　　　—Charles Spurgeon

Experience His glory:

Before we read the words of Jonathan Edwards, it's important for us to know that the account of this experience was found after he died. It is common for these guys to not talk about these experiences openly (Moody: "I hardly ever talk about.") That stands in stark contrast within certain parts of church culture where such experiences are much talked about because such experiences are considered the proof of being super spiritual.

31. Dwight L. Moody, "Crying for the Filling of the Holy Spirit," *Deeper Christian Quotes*, https://deeperchristianquotes.com/crying-for-the-filling-of-the-holy-spirit-dl-moody/.
32. "Reflection Guide: Ephesians 3:14–21," *Redemption Hill*, accessed February 27, 2022, https://redemptionhill.com/annyong/wp-content/uploads/2015/01/Ephesians3guide.pdf.
33. Ibid.

"Once, as I rode out into the woods for my health, in 1737, having alighted from my horse in a retired place, as my manner commonly has been, to walk for divine contemplation and prayer, I had a view that for me was extraordinary, of the glory of the Son of God, as Mediator between God and man, and his wonderful, great, full, pure and sweet grace and love, and meek and gentle condescension. This grace that appeared so calm and sweet, appeared also great above the heavens. The person of Christ appeared ineffably excellent, with an excellency great enough to swallow up all thought and conception — which continued, as near as I can judge, about an hour; which kept me the greater part of the time in a flood of tears, and weeping aloud. I felt an ardency of soul to be, what I know not otherwise how to express, emptied and annihilated; to lie in the dust, and to be full of Christ alone; to love him with a holy and pure love; to trust in him; to live upon him; to serve and follow him; and to be perfectly sanctified and made pure, with a divine and heavenly purity. I have several other times had views very much of the same nature, and which have had the same effects.[34]

—Jonathan Edwards

Edwards was suddenly so overwhelmed with the reality of the perfection, the purity, the magnitude of God's nature that this already godly man desired to be emptied and annihilated; to lie in the dust and be full of Christ alone; to love Him with a holy

---

34. Jonathan Edwards, *An Autobiography, a Personal Narrative, by Jonathan Edwards*, A Puritan's Mind, accessed February 27, 2022, https://www.apuritansmind.com/puritan-favorites/jonathan-edwards/biographical-writings/edwards-personal-narrative/.

and pure love; to trust in Him; to live upon Him; to serve and follow Him; and to be perfectly sanctified and made pure with a divine and heavenly purity. What he understood and believed about the glory of God in Scripture was brought to bear on him experientially.

Pascal, the famous French mathematician, intellectually understood the claims of the gospel. But in 1654, his faith moved from the abstract to a personal experience of Jesus. He wrote of that experience in his journal. After Pascal died, someone discovered that he had actually taken this journal entry and sewn it into his coat. Every time he bought a new coat, he took the journal entry out of the old coat and put it in the new coat so he would never be far from the remembrance of his experience. Here is some of what he wrote in that entry.

In the year of the Lord 1654, Monday, November 23 from about half-past ten in the evening until half-past twelve.

Fire
God of Abraham, God of Isaac, God of Jacob
Not of philosophers nor of the scholars.
Certitude. Certitude. Feeling. Joy. Peace.
God of Jesus Christ,
My God and thy God.
"Thy God shall be my God."
Forgetfulness of the world and of everything, except God. . . .
Joy, joy, joy, tears of joy.[35]

---

35. "Pascal's Coat," *Stories for Preaching*, accessed February 27, 2022, https://storiesforpreaching.com.au/sermonillustrations/pascals-coat/.

Notice how Pascal said, "not of philosophers." He had experienced *reality*, the absolute reality of Jesus, the absolute certainty of Jesus.

Edwards and Pascal are important to reference when we talk about these experiences because most people think such experiences are rooted in emotionalism. Christians and non-Christians alike recognize Edwards and Pascal as two of the greatest intellects in history. They were analytical, and they were rational. Pascal laid the groundwork for the entire field of probability statistics. These were not men prone to emotional excess.

Paul is not talking about emotionalism. He isn't talking about emotion for the sake of emotion. He isn't talking about seeking some ecstatic emotional experience. He is talking about the actual experience of the presence of Jesus, the actual experience of the love of Jesus, the actual experience of the fullness of God's glory. Yes! Every person's experience we just read included very real emotions, even very real physiological feelings that overcame them when they experienced the presence of Jesus, the love of Jesus, and the fullness of God's glory.

These moments and every resulting emotional and physical feeling that might accompany them are, however, not the basis of the Christian life. Here's why. We can never base our day-to-day walk with God on our feelings alone because not everything we feel is true. I might feel like someone doesn't like me when, in reality, they actually like me. And we don't always respond to our emotions in a proper way. Because of that, we need times that require faith without feelings. The Bible is replete with accounts of such times. There are so many accounts of people who experienced sustained times of spiritual dryness—times when the sense of God's favor was absent. David, the psalmist and shepherd king of Israel, is a prime example of this.

How long, O LORD? Will you forget me forever? How long will you hide your face from me? But I have trusted in your steadfast love; my heart shall rejoice in your salvation.

—Ps. 13:1, 5

How long, O LORD? Will you hide yourself forever? Lord, where is your steadfast love of old, which by your faithfulness you swore to David?

—Ps. 89:46, 49

It's only in those times of dryness and darkness that we learn certain things about our own heart. It's when God *feels* absent—when we don't *feel* His love and don't *feel* the weight of His glorious nature—that we learn to trust that He will never leave us or forsake us. We trust that He loves us and that He is perfectly just and holy in all His ways.

Paul's prayer doesn't contradict any of that. Paul said in his letter to the Galatians, "I have been crucified with Christ. It is no longer I who live, but Christ who lives in me. And the life I now live in the flesh I live by faith in the Son of God, who loved me and gave himself for me" (Gal. 2:20).

Looking back at what we've learned in this book on Ephesians 1–3, I have to take by faith all that God's Word says about who I am in Jesus. And in this second prayer, Paul wants us to know we can never become the person Jesus died for us to be without sometimes experiencing the actual presence of Jesus, the actual love of Jesus, and the actual fullness of God's glory.

Christians, we need to experience and expect times of dryness and darkness that reveal our hearts and require faith. But we also need to experience times when we experience the living, bright reality of Jesus. For us to navigate life well, we have to expect and experience both because that's the way life is. Neither should scare us.

Here's what *is* scary. Most churches emphasize one of these to their congregation but not usually both. Sadly, the emphasis of one without the other divides the church. Both camps look at the other with disdain, proud of their position and critical of the other's.

Paul was on his knees for these men and women. "For this reason I bow my knees before the Father" (Eph. 3:14). Many of them he had led to faith in Jesus. He was on his knees for men and women who already had Jesus living in them.

> *Paul here then is saying, "Christians, you know God loves you. I want you to be thunderstruck that God loves you. I want you to be conquered. I want you to be ambushed. I want you to be amazed."*[36]
> —Timothy Keller

The fact that Paul was on his knees praying for them tells us that they weren't usually experiencing these things and that it was important for them to experience the presence of Jesus, the love of Jesus, and the fullness of God's glory. I'm certain that the situation is the same for all of us. Many lack the experience of being in the presence of Jesus, of experiencing the love of Jesus and the fullness of God's glory. It's so important for every Christian to experience these things.

God was doing some amazing things in the early 1970s. People went everywhere telling people that they had met Jesus. They went everywhere telling people that Jesus loved them. And

---

36. Timothy J. Keller, *The Timothy Keller Sermon Archive, 1989–2015* Logos, accessed February 27, 2022, https://www.logos.com/product/148670/timothy-keller-sermon-archive-1989-2015.

many of them had barely read the Bible. Jesus was such a living, bright reality in the life of the person who had led me to Jesus that it was tangible! When that person said the name of Jesus, it was obvious that he knew Jesus personally.

Thousands of people were experiencing the reality of gospel theology before they knew where to find it in the pages of Scripture. I was a brand new Christian then, and I remember a Friday night sitting in a single-wide trailer that served as the library for a Catholic school in the city of Orange, California. That's where a handful of older men and women in that Catholic church met for prayer and to wait on the Lord. As I sat there, I had the experience of the reality of God's love. It was as if the finger of God touched my forehead and the love of God was poured into me. The flow of it reached into eternity. I had never read Jeremiah 31:3 where it says that God loves us with an everlasting love.

But here's the beautiful thing. Young men and women were showing up by the thousands to hear a man teach about the Jesus they had experienced. And they began to find the truth of Scripture that defined their experience. They couldn't wait to study the Bible because they wanted to learn more about the Jesus who was a living, bright reality to them and whose love and presence and glory were so real. There was no big production and no hype— just a middle-aged, balding man leading a few simple choruses a capella who, after 15 or 20 minutes of singing, would say, "Shall we turn in our Bibles to . . ." No one said we should come to church because they had Starbucks. No one said we should come because they had an amazing production or the services were short or the guy was funny. People invited people to hear about and meet Jesus, a living, bright reality!

Ask yourself this: what is the draw for going to church in modern church culture? How do they get people to come in the door? It is probably scores of things other than Jesus. When Jesus is a living, bright reality in the life of believers, Jesus will be the draw.

Do you see the need for the Holy Spirit to bring the experiential knowledge of the presence of Jesus, the love of Jesus, and the fullness of God's glory into your inner being?

epilogue

Paul's second prayer for the Christians in Ephesus (Eph. 3:14–21) is one of the most challenging passages of the Bible. It is challenging because it makes it clear that life as God intends it—the life Jesus died for us to have—is not outside-in; it is inside-out. It challenges the way the average churchgoer thinks about life. It challenges people who approach Christianity in the hopes of having their circumstances changed. It challenges ministers and ministries that frame the gospel as the way to change your circumstances.

But here's the thing. What Paul is praying for is outside the realm of any human effort. He says "that according to the riches of his glory he may grant you to be strengthened with power through his Spirit in your inner being" (Eph. 3:16). It's a work that only the Holy Spirit can do.

The entire Christian life is beyond a person's ability. Many people think they become a Christian by simply deciding to attach themselves to a subculture called Christianity. But being a Christian is a miracle! It is a human impossibility. It requires the work of the Holy Spirit revealing to us the truth about our sin. It requires the work of the Holy Spirit revealing to us the truth that Jesus is "the way, and the truth, and the life [and that] no one comes to the Father except through [Jesus]" (John 14:6) because Jesus is the Son of God who conquered our great enemies of sin and death when He died on the cross in our place for our sins and three days later rose from the grave.

Moralism appeals to the efforts of mankind. Being religious appeals to the efforts of mankind. Christianity makes no appeal to the moral or religious efforts of mankind. Brian Brodersen, pastor of Calvary Chapel Costa Mesa, said, "No good work will bring a dead spirit back to life." All we can do is believe all God has done to save us in the sending of His Son. At that moment, the Holy Spirit causes us to be born again and made alive to God.

There might be some readers who think that becoming a Christian is kind of like switching political parties—you come to agree with the moral values of people who call themselves Christian, you like the things they stand for, and you like being around them. I'm sure you know someone who thinks they're Christian for those same reasons. They don't talk much about Jesus, but they like the parts of the Bible that offer advice on how to have a better life. For them, church is inspirational. They like to hear messages that leave them feeling affirmed and empowered to go after life with a passion. Then there are those who have genuinely trusted in Jesus but still process gospel living as outside-in. They see the Bible as a book of advice—not just good advice but God advice intended to lift them up, inspire them, and fuel their passions.

Paul didn't say, "I'm on my knees in prison praying for you to have passion."

Passion = strong and barely controllable emotion; a thing arousing enthusiasm

No, Paul got on his knees in a Roman prison and prayed that the Holy Spirit would make the *presence* of Jesus, the *love* of Jesus, and the *fullness* of His glory a living, bright reality!

Jesus is the one who arouses enthusiasm. The word *enthusiasm* is based on the word *theos*, which means "God." In Latin and Greek, it originally meant "possessed by a god, inspired." Paul essentially prayed for the Christians in Ephesus to be possessed by the living, bright reality of the presence of love, the love of Jesus, and the glory of Jesus.

We've seen how the living, bright reality of the presence of Jesus, the love of Jesus, and the glory of Jesus can produce and be accompanied by emotional and even physiological responses. But Paul was not praying for the Holy Spirit to produce strong and barely controllable emotions. Human effort can provoke strong and barely controllable emotions. Art, music, literature, and movies can make you weep, make you laugh uncontrollably, and make you feel great. But no human effort can make Jesus a living, bright reality to us. Human effort can make church interesting or fun, and it can cause people to be excited about going to church. But it is the Holy Spirit alone working in the very center of a person's being who can make Jesus a living, bright reality to us.

We can't fabricate this work. This is more than goose bumps. This is not about trying to find the right song sung by the right singer supported by the right musicians in the perfect worship venue. This is not about inspirational personality. This is the work of the Holy Spirit! And I can use the word here—that work is His passion.

Here's how Martyn Lloyd-Jones speaks about that work of the Holy Spirit: "the truth begins to shine." The truth makes its way from the mind into the heart that you "may have strength to comprehend with all the saints what is the breadth and length and height and depth, and to know the love of Christ that surpasses knowledge, that you may be filled with all the fullness of God" (Eph. 3:18–19).

Comprehend = *katalambano* – usually means to be ambushed

Paul uses that word in 1 Thessalonians 5:4 (KJV): "But ye, brethren, are not in darkness, that that day should overtake you as a thief." There's our word—*katalambano*. You don't want to be ambushed by the day of the Lord. In Ephesians 3:18, Paul says it something like this: you understand that the gospel tells you Jesus loves you. I'm praying that you will be amazed, ambushed, overtaken, and utterly conquered by the reality of His love.

The Holy Spirit shines the truth into our inner being in a way that surprises us—ambushes us. Sometimes He does that when we are gathered and worshiping God in song. You're singing something you know to be true about God, but suddenly you're ambushed, overtaken, and utterly conquered by the reality of what you're singing. You *really* know that about Him.

Here's how one person spoke about the Holy Spirit making Jesus a living, bright reality. He said to think of a piece of photographic film (however, I'm not speaking as a professional photographer versed in the medium of film and developing that film). That film is chemically treated to make it sensitive to light. Light bounces off objects and comes in through the shutter and strikes the now-sensitized film. The result is that the light creates an image on that strip of film.

Our heart is the medium the Holy Spirit is working with. There are times when He has worked in our heart to sensitize our heart to the light of God's Word. And in that moment, the truth comes in and leaves us with a powerful, stunning, living reality of the presence of Jesus, the love of Jesus, and the glory of Jesus.

He does that not just to leave us thunderstruck and amazed. He brings into our inner being the living, bright reality of Jesus to change us, and our heart is changed and reformed, and the way we live changes.

A lot of people go to church and get emotional. That's okay, but I'm never going to tell you to be more emotional or to not be emotional. There's nothing wrong with emotion when it is in response to who God is and what God has done for you. There's nothing wrong with emotion when the Holy Spirit makes Jesus a living, bright reality to you. It may be impossible to not be overwhelmed with emotion when that truly happens. But there is something radically wrong if you're having an emotional experience at church and your life isn't changing. If that's the case, you are not experiencing the living, bright reality of Jesus. You're just being emotional.

There are a lot of people who keep coming back to church hoping to have another emotional experience because whatever it was they experienced the week before, they went out and fell back into sin or by mid-week felt discouraged, powerless, and hopeless. They're passionate about passion and felt passionate as they walked out the door, but they lost their passion by Tuesday. Every week is "rinse and repeat."

They're trying to find the musical performance, the live production, or the dynamic speaking that is motivational and produces emotions. Paul wasn't praying for that to happen because you can have all that going on and not ever experience the living, bright reality of the presence of Jesus, the love of Jesus, or the glory of Jesus.

Paul started his prayer like this: "For this reason I bow my knees before God" because of everything I've written to you about the gospel. He was essentially asking the Holy Spirit to help him preach the truth he'd written, about all that God has done in, with, through, and by Jesus. He was praying for the Holy Spirit to ambush them with the glorious gospel, cause them to come under the power of the gospel, and enable them to see Jesus, not with their physical eyes but with the eyes of their heart. He wanted them to "taste and see that the Lord is good!" (Ps. 34:8).

> The Christian life is never a matter of experience without truth.

But that's where a lot of people want to live, and there are plenty of churches that cater to them. There are churches that design their services to elicit an emotional response with little or no reference to the truth of Scripture. The tragedy is that they fail to see that the doctrine, the truth they so highly value, *should* move the human heart. They miss the biblical fact that those doctrines are the very means by which the Holy Spirit ambushes and overtakes the hearts of men and women.

LIVE AS THOUGH IT'S TRUE

I have been a Christian for 48 years, but I am discovering in the book Ephesians that my view of Christianity has been *so small*. My view of the gospel has been *so small*. I pray that this book written to first century Christians has amazed you with just how *big* the Gospel is. God wants you and me to *live big* in His *big Gospel*. He wants us to be free from the relentless task of trying to create an identity based on the shifting values of culture and the fickle approval of other broken humans. Our creator wants you and me to live in and live from everything He says about who we are in Jesus, with Jesus, through Jesus and by Jesus.

How do we do that? The one word answer is "faith." Faith is much more than mere cognitive agreement with what God says about our identity and who we are because of Jesus. It's not like reading, "he predestined us for adoption to himself as sons through Jesus Christ, according to the purpose of his will" (Ephesians 1:5) and checking the box that says "Yes, I believe that I'm the adopted child of God." The Bible says that we "live by faith" (Romans 1:17). In another place the author of Ephesians said "the life I now live I live by faith in the Son of God who loved me and gave Himself for me" (Galatians 2:20). I like to say that "faith is *living as though* what God has said is true." There are plenty of times when I don't *feel* like I'm the adopted child of God. There are plenty of times when I've messed up and I feel like God's probably doesn't want me as His adopted child anymore. Here's where faith comes in. God *said* that He predestined me to be His adopted child "through Jesus". Faith is going to live as though that's exactly who I am. When I was a young Christian, I was at a retreat where a speaker told a story that illustrates what faith looks like. That illustration has stayed with me for over forty years. The story involved a French tightrope walker and acrobat named Charles Blondin. Blondin toured the United States and was known for crossing the 1,100 ft (340 m) Niagra Gorge on a tightrope — more than once! On one occasion he crossed it pushing a wheelbarrow on a tightrope, 1,100 ft (340 m) long, 3.25 in (8.3 cm) in diameter and 160 ft (49 m) above the water, near the location of the current Rainbow Bridge. The story has it that before Blondin stepped onto the tightrope the crowds were placing bets on whether or not Blondin would succeed. One man in the crowd insisted that Blondin was the greatest tightrope artists of all time and that he was certain he would make it across the gourge. The story has it that the crowd said, "If you're truly believe Blondin is going to make it, don't bet your money, get into his wheelbarrow!" In other words, "Live as though you believe Blondin's the greatest."

Faith is getting into Jesus' wheelbarrow! Today, receive from Jesus the identity that you could never earn and never create!